Not Rocket Science

DADS

Mal Peachey

Not Rocket Science

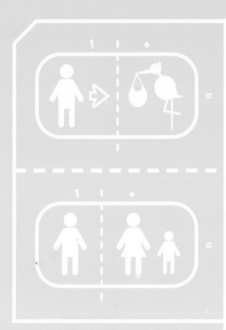

DADS

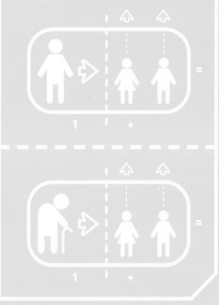

CASSELL
ILLUSTRATED

FIRST PUBLISHED IN GREAT BRITAIN IN 2005 BY CASSELL ILLUSTRATED
A DIVISION OF OCTOPUS PUBLISHING GROUP LIMITED
2–4 HERON QUAYS, LONDON E14 4JP

COPYRIGHT © 2005 ESSENTIAL WORKS LTD

CONCEPT, EDITORIAL, DESIGN AND LAYOUT BY ESSENTIAL WORKS LTD
168A CAMDEN STREET, LONDON NW1 9PT

THE MORAL RIGHT OF MAL PEACHEY TO BE IDENTIFIED AS THE AUTHOR
OF THIS WORK HAS BEEN ASSERTED IN ACCORDANCE WITH THE COPYRIGHT,
DESIGNS AND PATENTS ACT OF 1988

DISTRIBUTED IN THE UNITED STATES OF AMERICA BY
STERLING PUBLISHING CO., INC.
387 PARK AVENUE SOUTH, NEW YORK, NY 10016-8810

A CIP CATALOGUE RECORD FOR THIS BOOK IS AVAILABLE FROM THE BRITISH LIBRARY.

ISBN 1 84403 334 1
EAN 9781844033348

PRINTED IN CHINA

Contents

'Who of us is mature enough for offspring before the offspring themselves arrive? The value of marriage is not that adults produce children but that children produce adults.'

PETER de VRIES

7

Teenage kicks

8

We're not a happy family

9

We're a happy step-family

So, what's it all about?

To get things straight from the very beginning, this book is not about rocket science. There is nothing about quantum mechanics, the time-space continuum or the theory of relativity to be found here. So, what is it all about?

THE CLUE IS IN THE TITLE – DADS

The only stuff that you'll read within the pages of this book about mechanics will be with regard to your car. There is a lot of stuff about time (as in, finding it) and space. Specifically, creating more – because you're going to need it. However, the only hint of relativity will concern your relationships with your relatives.

This book is aimed at men, although it'll more than likely be bought by a woman to give to a man who is about to become, is considering becoming or has just become a father. That's not to exclude any fathers who might have a whole bunch of kids running around the place, it's just that after the first two you're unlikely to find either the time or the inclination to read a book like this. You'll know it all by then anyway (or at least think that you do).

SO, WHY HAS YOUR PARTNER BOUGHT YOU THIS BOOK?

Sitting there, thinking about fatherhood, everything seems fairly easy and sensible, doesn't it? You might even feel that you're ready for anything. But when the mother of your child is changing physically and emotionally and you're attempting to come to terms with the idea of all that responsibility – as well as trying to fathom what's happening

to your relationship – then you'll realize that you need help. Having said that, nothing that you read can ever fully prepare you for what is going to happen.

This book has been written to give you an idea of what a new father may have to face in the 21st century. It offers a general introduction to the idea of what it is to be a father and, therefore, a man. It is not an in-depth medical or psychological help book. While the basics of conception and the physical changes that will affect the mother of your child are included here, the details are not. There are a number of other books out there, written by sensible, well-qualified people, that give you all the stuff that your partner will need to know about pregnancy and birth. Don't worry about it, she'll have them by now and will probably already know great chunks by heart.

No, this book is just for you, the man. There may well be things contained in here that your partner won't like reading and there will certainly be things that you don't want to know, but you've decided to become a dad – and there really is no hiding now.

As the author I've taken a few liberties with your position as a prospective or new father – I've assumed, for instance, that you want to be one. If you don't, then you won't want to read this. You can go on living your life as a boy, but let me just tell you that you're missing out on one of the most difficult but greatest experiences in life. Maybe you'll come back when you want to be a man.

Does all this stuff about 'being a man' seem annoying or patronizing, even to you? If it does, well, tough. You're a man, get over it.

It seems to me (and I'm the writer) that the idea and the reality of being a man had escaped me until I became a father. Then I knew that I had to become one. I'm not talking about becoming what you think is a man, because you've probably only got your old man and a few sports or film star role models to base your ideas on. No, the fact is that once you become a father and begin to face up to the enormous responsibility that goes with it, then you will start to realize what it takes to truly be a man. And it doesn't mean running around the woods yelping and wearing little in the way of clothing.

So, in this book you will find a lot of my opinions and also plenty of sensible advice (mostly gleaned from listening to sensible people) on how to deal with what can happen when you become a dad. And because there's a whole lot more living to do after the baby's first year, I've included chapters on some of the things that can, and all too often do, happen to families. I'm not suggesting that you will ever contemplate divorce (Chapter 8) or becoming a stepfather (Chapter 9), but you will certainly have to deal with being the father of teenagers (Chapter 7).

Given that by the time your kids become teenagers you'll have lost this book, the teen years chapter is mainly there to scare you. And help you to understand the importance of communication between you and your child throughout that child's life. While many people will not like this, I truly believe that the best way to keep your relationship with your children open, loving and working is to always be there for them, no matter what. Accept that your teenage son or daughter is going to have sex and experiment with weird fashions and drugs. And then let them do it all in their, i.e. your, home – that way you can always be there to help if things go wrong. Surprisingly, things rarely do go wrong, especially if your children have grown up knowing that you love them, appreciate them and respect them, too.

So, you may well ask, what makes me qualified to write this book? The answer is not much. Just that I had a father, I am a father and I know lots of fathers. And I have a lot of strong opinions about this stuff. I'm not a qualified anything and can't spout academic research or arcane 'findings'. Which, hopefully, you will appreciate. I hope that this book is entertaining and useful to you. I hope that you enjoy it.

Most importantly for me (and I'm the writer, remember?), I hope that this book confirms for you that the choice you've made in becoming a father is one of the most important, rewarding and wonderful that you are ever going to make.

Becoming a dad is not rocket science, it just feels that way sometimes.

Note Sometimes I refer to your child as she/her when the advice or examples apply to both genders. This is simply to avoid clumsiness and repetition.

Hello
Dad

WELCOME TO THE WEIRD AND WONDERFUL WORLD OF PARENTHOOD. DO BE SCARED, DO THINK TWICE AND DO ASK QUESTIONS. DON'T THINK ABOUT YOURSELF, THINK ONLY OF THE MOTHER OF YOUR CHILD AND THE NEW LIFE THAT YOU STAND EVERY CHANCE OF RUINING – WHICH YOU WILL IF YOU'RE A CRAP FATHER. SO, DON'T BE A BAD DAD, READ THIS, ABSORB, ARGUE AND ACT AS YOU THINK BEST.

Are you sure about this?

So, you want to be a dad. Are you sure? Are you really sure that you want to become a father? Because it's not like you're just changing jobs or cars. It's not like going to university, becoming an adult or making love with someone new. It is much, much more complicated and permanent than that.

Until now you've been you – as defined by what you like, what you wear, what job you do, what sports you play and follow, what music you listen to, how and what you drive, who your partner/lover/wife is. There's also your family – you're a son, possibly a brother, uncle, cousin. All of that has been easy to become, effortless really. But this is different. It's new, it's big, it's grown-up and it has to be clever.

Hello Dad!

THE MIRROR TEST

Stand in front of a mirror and look at yourself for at least 60 seconds. Now say to yourself, 'Hello Dad'. How does it feel?

- If it feels weird then that's good.
- If you feel excited that's also good.
- If you feel good, then enjoy it.
- If you feel scared, then that's very good. You should be scared, because we're all scared of what we don't know.
- If you feel apprehensive, get used to it.
- If you feel nothing, try it again. If you still feel nothing, come back when you're sober or have come down and try again.
- If, however, you feel depressed, stop right now. Try again tomorrow. If you still feel depressed then go to the second set of results below.

THE RESULTS

1 If you can combine feeling weird, scared, excited and good when you think of becoming a father, then you're starting out in a positive way. Becoming and being a dad is weird, scary, exciting and very, very good. It is also full of the unexpected, both good and bad unexpected, which is where this book will come in useful.

2 If you feel depressed, even after a couple of days of trying, then this is not the time for you to read this book. Hey, it's your life and you make the decisions. It might not be the right time for you yet, but that doesn't rule out fatherhood altogether, does it? Although it's OK if it does. Whatever, good luck and enjoy. Just make sure that the woman in your life knows about it and accept that you may have a lot of short-term relationships unless you find a woman to love who feels the same way about being a mother as you do about being a father. You're missing out on one of the greatest experiences life has to offer.

Becoming and being a dad is weird, scary, exciting and very, very good.

Be sure

If the mirror test has come out on the positive side, you can make absolutely sure that you want to do this by asking a further six, basic questions of yourself.

1 Can you forget about romantic weekends away for the next five years?

2 Can you function at work on less than five hours' sleep a night?

3 Can you forgo sexual relations with another woman, even when you're not having them with the mother of your child?

4 Can you imagine what changing a nappy is like?

5 Can you keep your calm when a small child is screaming, writhing on the floor and telling you that they hate you?

6 Can you lose that sports car (or not get one for the next 15 years or so)?

If you answered Yes to all of these questions then you are sure ... and you are ready to become a dad.

If you answered Yes to three or more then you'll be ready for fatherhood soon enough.

If you answered No to two or more then come back in a few years.

If you answered No to all these questions then go back to reading *FHM* or *Maxim* magazine.

Is she sure about this?

So you've discussed the idea of having a baby and she says she wants to. You've done your mirror test and come up in favour. And you've discussed with her the immediate future, right? She's accepted that she is to forsake all others excepting you (and you've promised likewise), whether you marry or not.

You both have to understand that when she's pregnant she stops being herself and becomes something wholly different, that she becomes a mother even though there's no sign of the impending birth.

She must know that you, the father-to-be of her child, is going to be with her every day for the rest of her life (don't even think of that not being the case at the moment). She understands that as well as all of the exciting presents, parties and joy coming her way, there is about to be a complete life change for both of you. Your job won't be as heavily affected, though of course there will be adjustments to be made to your working patterns, but hers will be a different matter altogether (more of that later).

She understands that she's going to be doing things for two for at least nine months, right? She needs to be sure she can look into the near future and see her stomach growing, her emotions being torn up, her eating habits altering and her body being prodded and probed by a line of doctors and nurses, and be happy about it.

If your partner feels OK about all the above, then it's time for her to take the mirror test, too. She has to say, 'Hello Mum', of course. The results for her stand exactly as they do for you.

Calculating the true cost of love.

Till death us do ...

It's worth discussing the marriage question at this stage if you are not already married (to each other, preferably), not least because wedding gifts can help a lot – the equipment needed to raise a child can be very expensive. Such a discussion can also help both of you think about spending many years together as parents, lovers and spouses.

Be sure – for her

Six questions for her to answer

1 Do you look forward to being called 'Mum'?

2 Do you look at mothers with children and think how good it will be?

3 Can you look at the intended father of your child and trust him, implicitly?

4 Do you mind if your career stalls for a while?

5 Can you keep your calm when a small child is screaming, writhing on the floor and telling you that they hate you?

6 Are you prepared for friendships with pals who have no children to cool?

If she answered Yes to all of these questions then she is sure ... and she is ready to become a mum.

If she answered Yes to three or more then she'll be ready for motherhood soon enough.

If she answered No to two or more then she should come back in a few years.

If she answered No to all these questions I don't believe you and you're just saying that because you said No.

If you're both sure about becoming parents, read on.

... at times like this, she might cry. Do not worry. This is a GOOD THING.

If you can witness her mirror test it might make you feel as happy as she's going to be (or not). Because women are usually not as good at hiding their emotions as men at times like this, she might cry. Do not worry. This is a GOOD THING. Crying for her is like leaping in the air and waving your arms about are for you at a game. If, on the other hand, a single tear falls without any other sign of emotion on her face, then that is probably not good. Unless you're the depressed-at-being-a-dad guy, in which case it's very good.

It's all in the planning

You are both sure that you want to start a family, so you just go ahead and get pregnant, right?

Becoming parents isn't as simple as getting married or moving house (although apparently it's far less stressful). Firstly, there's no guarantee you'll conceive immediately – many couples struggle to obtain a positive result for a year or longer (for more on that, see page 22). And then a Catch-22 kicks in, as the stress of trying to conceive can itself prevent this from happening. Other stresses in your life, from work, friends and things in general, can also prevent conception. In fact worries of any kind tend to work against you making babies. So stop worrying and help yourself to stop worrying by planning for your life after conception.

MONEY

Ask yourself if you are in a financial position that is conducive to beginning a family. You don't need stocks and shares and a mansion to bring children into the world, but it's a good idea to know what you do have. Look at how much you earn at present. Don't combine both your incomes, because the

The size of the pile of money each child costs grows exponentially as they do. (The money here is fake.)

mother will most likely be earning only part of her wage once she's on maternity leave and might not ever earn as much again once she is a mother. Look carefully at how you spend your money and think about what is going to change. Use these questions to help you plan:

- Do you have a pay rise pending? If so, what is it likely to be?

- Is your home big enough for a family of three? If not, how much can you afford to spend on a new place?

- Do you need to spend money decorating, building or altering your home? If so, where is the money coming from?

- How much do you spend on leisure? This is one of the few costs that will actually go down since you won't be eating out, going to clubs and indulging in nefarious night-time activities as much as you used to. And if you think that you will be, then you're in the wrong place.

- Is there a realistic possibility of taking a better-paid job?

And remember ...

DO NOT GAMBLE

It's a good rule for life in general but an essential one for a man about to take on immense responsibility.

DO NOT ENTER INTO A LIFE OF CRIME

At your age, it's ridiculous. And do you want your children to grow up not knowing who their father is/was? You'll get caught.

ACCOMMODATION

Presuming you're going to live together as a family unit, you'll need to make sure where you live is big enough for all of you. That will mean at least two bedrooms. Although the baby will sleep in the same room as its mother for the first few months, it's a good idea to get the child into a separate room as soon as possible. You might also find that useful if you need to sleep through the night or the day while the baby's awake.

... she may want to decorate the new home in a bizarre manner. This is due to her taste faculty being screwed up by pregnancy.

If you're considering moving home in order to accommodate your new family, make sure that you're in place before the baby is due. Ideally plan to move before the mother is into the final three months of her pregnancy (see box, page 47). Moving house is stressful and can adversely affect a pregnant woman. Oh, and beware, she may want to decorate the new home in a bizarre manner. This is due to her taste faculty being screwed up by pregnancy.

Make sure that your home is easily accessible for a pushchair, and parents carrying lots of bags and a baby, and that it is connected to all major services such as electricity, running water and so on.

Do not attempt to raise a child in a covered wagon or remote cabin.

WORK

Aside from the money issue (see above), you need to assess how your chances of promotion and thus upping your earning capacity will be affected by having a family. Find out if your employer allows any paid paternity leave (see page 119) and if they approve of employees taking it up. Yes, I know it's the law in the UK, but sadly that doesn't mean it's something that goes down well with all bosses.

Find out how much maternity leave your partner's employer allows, how much they pay and if they approve of employees taking it up. Again, it's the law in the UK, but …

Discuss with your partner whether she will want to go back to work after becoming a mother. She won't really know until she's had the baby, but you should discuss it now in principle anyway. And

don't hold her to what she says now. She's entitled to change her mind.

Find out if your or your partner's employee medical care covers dependants.

THE BIG EVENT

Detailed planning for the birth can be found later in this book, but initial planning involves deciding which hospital or clinic you will be using for tests, check-ups and so on, and getting a support group on board ready to be mobilized during the birth. Family is best, but neighbours and good friends can also be of great help. If you aren't able to drive, arrange with a neighbour or friend to make the dash to the maternity ward when the time comes.

Read this book

Test your dad potential

What kind of dad will you be? And should you be one in the first place? This simple test is designed to assess just how ready you are and may ever be for it. See page 67 for your results.

ROLE MODEL

As a child, you thought that your father was:

a Who?

b That bloke who used to come around Friday nights smelling of beer and spend the weekend sleeping on the sofa.

c A strict disciplinarian. I still call him 'Sir'.

d A nice guy who found it hard to talk to me but was 'always there' if I wanted to.

e My best mate growing up and still is.

f My dad.

These days you see your dad:

a Who?

b Never.

c At precisely the same time and place every week.

d Whenever Mum comes over or invites me there.

e He lives with me.

f When we feel like it.

What phrase best describes your mother:

a Who?

b The bitch from hell with too many boyfriends.

c She who must be obeyed.

d Cuddly.

e The kind of woman I'm going to marry.

f My mum.

ABOUT YOU

You're looking forward to being a dad because:

a Who's becoming a dad?

b Tried everything else.

c Your dad told you to.

d It's a nice idea and children are so cute.

e It'll be nice for your parents to have some grandchildren.

f You feel ready, your relationship is the right one, you're looking forward to the challenge.

Which of these words best describes you:

a Hard.

b Lad.

c Son.

d Cuddly.

e Fun.

f Reasonable.

Which car would you choose:

a Semi-truck.

b BMW convertible.

c Humvee.

d Beetle.

e MINI.

f Subaru.

You would like to live in:

a A trailer.

b A loft.

c A barracks.

d At home.

e Anywhere with a gym, bar, sauna, games facility.

f A house.

YOUR CHILDREN

Which statement best describes your thoughts on having a child:

a Ain't no child of mine.

b It won't change anything.

c Spare the rod and spoil the child.

d Can't wait to have someone to hug all the time.

e It's another generation of our family.

f It's going to be tough but fun (I hope).

How much time a week should you spend with your children?

a What children?

b Depends what time I get home.

c An hour a day.

d Whatever they want.

e More when they can start joining in things with adults.

f As much as possible given the work schedule of myself and my partner.

How much time should you spend with the mother of your child:

a Who?

b Depends what time I get home.

c Exactly as much time as my schedule allows.

d Whatever she says.

e We should always be together.

f When the time is right we should have one night a week together, alone.

DISCIPLINE

As a child, when you did something that you shouldn't have were you:

a Ignored for days on end.

b Made to sit in a bath of bleach for two days.

c Given six of the best.

d Given a disappointed look.

e Cuddled and told not to worry.

f Told what you'd done wrong and punished. You think.

Your schooldays were:

a What schooldays?

b Torture.

c Full of rules to be obeyed.

d The best days of my life.

e Fun, fun, fun.

f Some good, some bad.

You are told by your child's playgroup that your child is ordering other kids around. Do you:

a Ask what kid.

b Tell the playgroup to sort it out, that's why you send your child there.

c Give your child six of the best.

d Feel guilty.

e Ask to sit in playgroup for a week with your child.

f Discuss with the playgroup why it might be happening and ask for suggestions on how to stop it.

Your child's school has informed you that your child is mixing with a group that bullies other children. Do you:

a Ask what kid.

b Tell the school it's their problem, your child doesn't bully anyone at home.

c Give your child six of the best.

d Cry.

e Ask to attend school with your child.

f Speak to your child about their bullying friends and ask if they are scared of their friends, and work with the school to solve the problem.

The science of conception

You probably learned all about the birds and the bees at school – possibly in biology class, but more likely you had a rudimentary illustrated introduction to how babies are made in the bushes around the grounds with that dirty little boy in the year above who stole his big brother's magazine. So you know that the process of human conception is a fascinating and wondrous thing. This is how it's done.

In basic terms, when a male sperm meets a female egg in the body of the mother, they flirt, fall in love and get together, forming a single unit. Then they take a little journey together, when they start dividing themselves until they make a new human being. Sounds simple, right? Wait till you try it.

HIS JOB

Your contribution to pregnancy is all in your balls. From puberty onwards men produce sperm under orders from a mixture of testosterone in the testes and luteinizing hormone and follicle-stimulating hormone in the pituitary gland. From then on, for some of us it never stops. The great American writer Saul Bellow fathered a child with his 30-something wife when he was 86.

Each of the tiny little tadpole-like sperm that are produced in their millions every day are a 20th of a millimetre long, with a

The sperm's journey

Once released and on their way, your sperm travel together up through what's called the vas deferens, around your bladder and into your prostate. They mix with fluids from the vas deferens, prostate and other glands to make what we know as seminal fluid. At the prostate the ejaculatory duct joins the urethra through which the semen is ejected – often sooner than many of us want them to, but what the hell, in this instance we want it there, right?

BLADDER

VAS DEFERENS

PROSTATE

URETHRA

RECTUM

TESTIS

darkish head full of genetic data and a long tail that performs the swimming motion needed to carry it up, up and away. The tail and head are joined at a body section that produces the energy needed for the swim.

HER JOB

A woman has her full stock of eggs by the time she's born. These are then released at regular, monthly intervals between puberty and menopause. About 500 eggs are matured and released by a woman's ovaries during her fertile years. Every month an ovum is released from a different ovary (there are two, either side of the pelvis) and during this ovulation period a woman is at her most fertile – it lasts for between half a day and a day only. The egg sits in its fallopian tube awaiting the arrival of your sperm in order that they can make your baby.

MIGHTY MITE!

Your sperm might be too small to see without the aid of a powerful microscope, but he's a powerful little fella, no mistaking. And determined. He has to be, because it's a wonder that any children are born at all, given the precarious fate of the majority of your sperm. The vagina is full of very unfriendly acids that slow many of your plucky spermatozoa from continuing their onward journey (travelling normally at a rate of 2 or 3 million a minute). So it's no wonder that a lot less than the original 700 million sperm ejaculated get anywhere near the fallopian tube. Even once they make it they might choose the wrong tube, since only one holds the lucky, receptive egg ripe for fertilization. The journey through the fallopian is as tricky as any rocky pass through bandit country, since it's filled with more acids

See how amazing your sperm is? It's tiny, ugly and resembles a tadpole. Yet it's ready to fight all and anything thrown at it to make a baby.

(though less than in the vagina) and cleansing cells. And then the egg is not always easy to find …

But if you're lucky …

RESULT!!

When your mighty sperm and her egg meet and become cosy, they start splitting off and form a solid bunch of cells called a morula. These then divide and become a hollow ball of cells called a blastocyst, which then implants itself into the uterus lining. This is where the blastocyst becomes an embryo and starts knitting a placenta in order to support the embryo's growth and connect it to the mother's support system. Congratulations. You've made a baby. Wasn't that hard, was it?

But we're getting ahead of ourselves here …

How to do it naturally

Now you're ready to start making babies, there's nothing to worry about, right? You probably think that this is the easy and fun part. Have sex as often as possible without any protection and it'll happen. Well, maybe. But maybe not. Generally accepted statistics show that among couples having unprotected sex:

- a quarter will conceive within a month
- just over half will conceive within 6 months
- three-quarters will conceive within 9 months
- 90% will conceive within 18 months

However, that's assuming that both of you are within touching years of your peak

Enjoy your mission!

| Think about making things seem spontaneous and get her to surprise you with her advances.

| Use sexual role-playing games if you both like that.

| Make sure you are both as relaxed as possible while making love and see the event as something to look forward to rather than to endure. It'll make all the difference.

You'll see a lot of these – a pregnancy test kit.

fertility age, which is 24. In reality, these days the chances are increasingly that neither of you can remember much about having been 24 apart from a few embarrassing snogs and almost as many embarrassing nights. If you're older (and you probably are) the chances of a quick conception recede.

Look at those figures again. Only *one in four* couples will have success immediately, you're on an almost 50:50 chance of success within six months, but you may well take longer than that to achieve pregnancy. The longer you both go without lighting up the blue pregnancy test paper, the more you're going to feel pressured and stressed about it, and then you'll start trying out bizarre and sometimes ridiculous 'fertility' aids. Before

The 28-day menstrual cycle

Yes, of course, it's all women's stuff, isn't it? But in this case the intricacies of the menstrual cycle are worth getting your head round – it's the key to giving you and your partner every possible chance of successful conception.

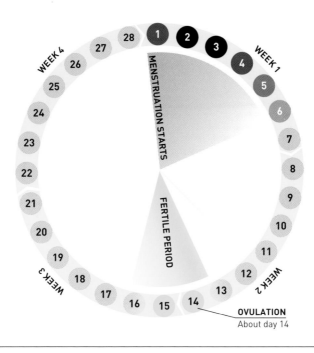

MENSTRUATION STARTS

FERTILE PERIOD

WEEK 4

WEEK 1

WEEK 2

WEEK 3

OVULATION
About day 14

you know it you're blaming each other for her not becoming pregnant and it's all going wrong. You didn't want to be a dad anyway ...

Hang on, stop. Don't go there. It ain't necessarily so. Armed with enough information about what can really help with conception you can seriously increase your chances of a positive result.

TIMING

The optimum time for a woman to conceive is during that important 12- to 24-hour period after ovulation has occurred. Ovulation always happens at 14 days before the end of her menstruation cycle. So that should be easy, shouldn't it? Of course it's not. Despite a woman technically having a 28-day menstruation cycle, there are often variations. For a number of reasons, among them the stress generated by the desire to be pregnant, a menstruation cycle can be shorter or longer than the standard four weeks. In addition, if a woman has been taking a contraceptive pill prior to deciding to try for a baby, then her body will take some time to return to a 'natural' menstruation cycle, that is, one dictated by her own hormones and not those sent by the Pill. Problems at work, overeating or drinking, and arguments with you, the prospective father of her child, can all alter the menstrual cycle, thus throwing into confusion the precise 14th day before the end of the cycle and thus the time of ovulation.

In other words, it is not always easy for a woman to reasonably predict the date of her ovulation. When she can (or even thinks that she can), you have to be ready to perform. So don't be on a business trip away from home, don't arrange a boys' night out, pass on those tickets for the game and be ready, willing and able to set the miracle of creation into motion.

PSYCHOLOGY

Is there anything about the previous section that bothered you? You're sure the idea of 'performing on demand' isn't a problem at all? Being a man, you probably like to think that you're in control, that you call the shots and that you decide when (and where) you're going to have sex. Sorry, but until this mission is accomplished, you can forget all that. You will have sex when and where she says. That means being on call for a matter of four or five days around the time of her ovulation, ready and able to put your sperm

> ## A woman who is determined to have a baby can think of only that. It is a task to be done ...

in touch with her egg. Which isn't very romantic, is it?

It'll probably surprise you to discover that when it comes to procreation females aren't necessarily the more romantic sex. A woman who is determined to have a baby can think of only that. It is a task to be done and she can't do it without you (thankfully), in much the same way that you can't fix a leaking sink without a wrench.

Unsurprisingly, a man who has to consider that he is nothing more than a wrench can feel kind of low. In every sense. Which is where the psychology comes in. You have to forget about becoming a father and think only of the sex. It used to be easy, it shouldn't be too difficult now. She can help a lot here but you need to discuss it with her first.

If you begin to find it difficult to perform on demand, you could ask that the demand be couched in more alluring terms than simply getting a call that says, 'I'm ovulating, got to do it now'. If, on the other hand, that's stimulating enough, you're a lucky guy.

SMOKING

Don't be stupid. You should have given up years ago. Put it out and get off the nicotine. It badly affects your health at every level, including sperm production. It also adversely affects those close to you inasmuch as they inhale your stale smoke, have to put up with your stinking breath and feel like they live in an ashtray. If you smoke and you've got this far in a relationship with a woman who wants to have your baby then the chances are that she smokes too. Great. You can either both suffer, stink and reduce your chances of getting pregnant (or, if you do achieve it, increase the risk of your baby being born

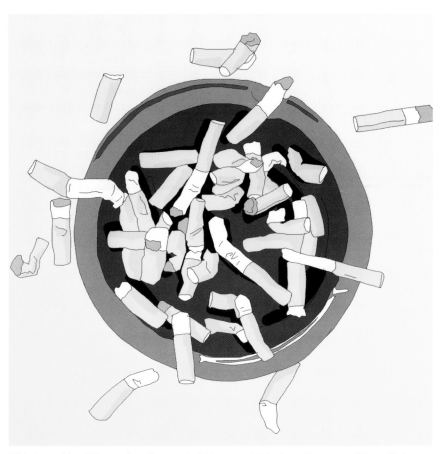

If this is your idea of the morning after a good night, you need to try hypnotism or something radical.

deformed and addicted to nicotine), or you can quit together. Then you can live longer lives together and have a healthy baby.

DRINK

You probably drink at least the internationally recognized maximum weekly amounts of alcoholic units. That's 21 average-sized glasses of wine, or about 10 pints of beer, 12 decent cocktails but as many as 210 lite beers (that's a joke, but only just). But you probably drink that much over a weekend or even in one night. If you are aged under 30, it's highly likely that you will drink much more than 21 units of alcohol a week. And it's still likely that you'll exceed the amount if you're aged between 30 and 40. You're a guy, it's what you do.

We all know why we drink so much. Apart from enjoying the taste and the camaraderie that goes with social drinking, alcohol is a relaxant, it's an uninhibitor, it

Sign of a good night in? Not for your sperm, let alone your head . . .

makes you witty and clever and brave. You probably think that it can make you feel horny because past experience has suggested that this is the case. When you were single you would go out for the night, have a few drinks, go to a club, meet a woman who found you as witty, clever and brave as you felt and, if all went well, you'd go back to your place or hers and have sex. The next day you'd both feel a little hungover, happy but vague.

Happy days, eh? No, quite.

As you have undoubtedly discovered to your regret, alcohol can make you incapable of performing sexually. Sometimes it all begins well enough only for something to switch off halfway through the act and the action to go, ahem, limp.

And there's more bad news. Alcohol damages your semen production. If you've read the bit on page 22 about how difficult it really is for your sperm to get to mission accomplished, you'll understand that it needs all the help it can get.

So don't drink too much while you're trying to become a dad. It really doesn't help. And it doesn't make you witty, clever or brave either. A few drinks are OK, so try to keep within the 21-units limit and you'll increase your chances of being relaxed, uninhibited and able to perform properly. And in case you were thinking that a few cups of coffee after drinking might help sober you up and improve your fertility, don't. Coffee doesn't sober you up, it simply raises your pulse rate and can make you feel temporarily revived, but it's just as likely to increase your need to urinate at the wrong time. Plus,

coffee is bad for your sperm too, since it depletes your natural supplies of zinc and folic acid (as does alcohol), both of which are very important for making babies.

DRUGS

That's the illegal kind, the sort that you may have flirted with in your youth but that you'd never think of touching now, would you?

CLASS A SUBSTANCES

That's cocaine, heroin, Ecstasy, LSD, amphetamines and other assorted chemically derived opiates, hallucinogenics and expensive brain burners sold by men you wouldn't invite to your baby's first birthday party. If you want to conceive a child do not touch these substances. If you want to remain at liberty do not buy these drugs. If you want to grow up and be a father just say no to these substances. But then, you knew that.

CANNABIS

Since you know that a glass of wine a day can improve a woman's chances of conceiving, you can probably work out that a little cannabis may well have the same effect. Certainly it's a relaxant, similarly it has far fewer health-damaging side-effects than alcohol. However, smoking it in a joint means taking tobacco and nicotine with tar into your body, which is not good. Inhaling anything other than oxygen into your lungs is generally to be avoided. Hash cookies can have a similar result with far less damaging side-effects. Too many can lead to an increase in body fat, which isn't nice, but that can easily be controlled.

So the biggest problem of using cannabis as an aid to conception is the threat that buying or growing it has on your

Alcohol and pregnancy

A Danish survey on fertility, published in 2001 and conducted on almost 40,000 pregnant women, found that those who drank a glass of wine a day were more likely to become pregnant more quickly than those who drank over that amount, and even sooner than women who didn't drink at all. The researcher, Mette Juhl, concluded, 'Small amounts of alcohol may have a positive impact on the female reproductive system, perhaps by helping women to feel more relaxed.' She could not claim that alcohol would actually improve a woman's fertility, but rather that 'a moderate intake may correlate with a higher frequency of intercourse, which may explain the longer waiting times in women who reported no intake'.

So chill with a glass of wine and let nature take its course.

freedom. While in certain countries it's no longer considered a criminal offence to be stopped by law enforcement agents with a few grams of the stuff on you, it is still illegal to deal in it. Which means that you have to break the law and mix with people who break the law for a living in order to get it. That is a matter for you.

PRESCRIPTION DRUGS

If either you or your partner is taking any prescription drugs while attempting to conceive a child, you should consult your doctor about their possible effect on your chances of success.

ALTERNATIVE MEDICINE

There are a number of vitamin tablets, dietary supplements and homeopathic pills that can help make your sperm strong and active. Take extra doses of **vitamins B12**, **E** and **C** and, on the mineral side, take **zinc** (30mg) and **copper** (1mg), and consider taking **folic acid** tablets, since drink depletes your levels of this mineral. Both **carnitine** and **arginine** are considered to have a positive effect on sperm mobility and can be purchased in pill form. They can be added to a mixture of **taurine**, **selenium**, **ginseng**, **ginkgo**, **nutmeg** and **ashwagandha** to create an apparently potent alternative cocktail, designed to get your pecker up and keep it there.

DIET

As popular opinion would have it, you are what you eat. Since what you put into your body affects what comes out of it, your child is going to be what you eat, too. Do you want your baby to be a hotdog, burger or bundle of fries? If you answered yes to that question you are an idiot.

Food, glorious food

If you look on your quest to conceive as a marathon then you need to train and prepare for it. These are some of the best foods you can eat to aid good health, fertility and a long life.

Water Drink lots of it, every day. Some 'experts' recommend at least 2 litres a day, others 4 litres. Whatever the amount, it's definitely worth replacing some daily coffee intake with water.

Fruit Apples, kiwis, cherries, raspberries, bananas, oranges, blueberries, strawberries, mangoes and avocados. Dried fruits are particularly good for her because they're full of iron.

Vegetables The superveg are broccoli, kale and tomatoes. Pretty much any other vegetable is going to do you some good, just don't overcook it because that kills all the vitamins and good stuff in it. Green veg are particularly good for you, bursting with iron and other vitamins and minerals, just like your mum said.

Meat Chicken without the skin, red meat in moderation (as long as it's good quality and not fried), liver, game and high-quality sausages are good for you. Hotdog sausages from a can or street vendor are not. A homemade burger using good-quality, lean beef is OK and full of protein.

Fish Oily fish like salmon, mackerel, tuna and sardines are really good for you. Grill, bake or poach them. White meaty fish are also good. In fact, any fish is good, as long as it's not deep-fried or boiled into a mash. Shellfish can be high in cholesterol, so check your levels first. Try to eat at least one fish dish a week, ideally two.

Oil Whenever possible, use olive oil, good-quality vegetable oil or nut oil. Do not use any margarines that contain trans-fats in cooking or in sandwiches. Use butter if you must, but sparingly.

Pulses & nuts Rice, lentils, couscous and all types of dried beans are very good for your digestive system. So are wholegrain breads (particularly rye) and pasta. As with any food, the rule is not to eat too much of any one type. Nuts are good, as long as they're not salted or coated in sugar. Particularly good for heart and sexual performance are walnuts, brazil nuts and almonds.

Food is not just your source of fuel that keeps you going; it dictates how you keep going and for how long. You must have either been told or read somewhere by now that there are foods that are very bad for you, despite tasting good. All fast food is soaked in fat, sugar, salt and who knows what else. Look what deep-fried peanut butter sandwiches did for Elvis – he died aged 40, sitting on the toilet.

Hopefully you'll know something about your family health history and whether the male line of your family has suffered from congenital heart disease or any other life-threatening disorder. If you don't know then get your cholesterol, lipid and liver function tested by your doctor as soon as possible. It doesn't hurt and can add many years to your life. If you've got a problem then the doc will help with drugs and serious dietary advice. If there's no obvious danger at present, keep it that way by eating sensibly and exercising regularly.

Getting juicy

Buy a cool-looking electric juicer and make your own smoothies and juices. Not only will this save you money in the long run, but it will allow you to be confident that there are no unwanted ingredients (most often sugar) added to the mix. It's the quickest way for your body to process all the good stuff in fruit.

Look what deep-fried peanut butter sandwiches did for Elvis – he died aged 40, sitting on the toilet.

How to do it with help

If after a while – probably 18 months or so – you are still having no luck conceiving and neither of you knows of any reason why it's not working, then you should seek professional help. There'll undoubtedly be friends and aged relatives who can and will make ludicrous suggestions, such as standing on your head after sex, or eating raw eggs, milk and bull sperm for breakfast, to help with conception. Most of these will be of no help at all. They might be fun, but scientifically and practically they're highly unlikely to have any effect on your chances of conceiving. So what can you do?

THE SPERM TEST

The purpose of the test is to see if your sperm is strong enough and willing enough to do the job asked of it. It also checks whether you have enough sperm.

You can ask your partner's gynaecologist for advice on where to have the test, or you can arrange to visit a clinic via your doctor. You will be expected to provide a fresh sample of sperm. It's unlikely that you'll be able to produce the sample at home and carry it with you to the clinic (it has to be warm and freshly secreted), so you'll be asked to visit a room or lavatory to do this. Not all such clinics provide visually stimulating material to help you, so you may want to take your own.

HER TESTS

Because a woman is a more complicated being than a man, or at least her reproductive system is, there are many more things that can go wrong. While you just have to put some sperm into a pot, there are a number of far more involved tests that can be carried out on your partner in order to ascertain whether she has a medical problem that is preventing her from conceiving.

Her doctor may suggest that she undergoes a series of tests to determine whether she has any serious problems. The tests could be any of the following:

- **hormone and ovulation tests** – to measure the hormone levels in her blood and urine every day for a month

- **ultrasound scan** – to check the health of her ovaries

- **endometrial biopsy** – a slightly more intrusive procedure, to check the health of her uterus. A tiny part of her uterus is taken and examined during the second half of her menstrual cycle

- **hysterosalpingogram** – to check for any blockages. Her uterus and tubes are filled with a dye that shows up under X-ray. If the dye fails to enter a tube then the tube is blocked

- **laparoscopy** – to check her fallopian tubes. A viewing tube is inserted through her abdomen in order to see if the tubes are blocked or twisted. This is done under general anaesthetic

WHAT IS IVF?

IVF stands for In Vitro Fertilization, which translates as in glass (*in vitro*) fertilization.

It's the method of combining male sperm with female eggs to create an embryo, which is then reinserted into the mother's womb for the normal term of pregnancy. Although the process is a proven fertility treatment, it isn't 100% successful.

WHAT IF IVF FAILS?

If your tests reveal that you or your partner – or possibly both – is physically not able to have children, this does not mean that you cannot have a family.

- **You can adopt a child** In the UK, the rules and regulations governing the adoption of children can be difficult to overcome and can vary between counties and local authorities. There will be a local adoption agency near you that will be able to give you all the necessary information regarding the process.

- **You can adopt from abroad** Since a devastating governmental policy that rewarded the birth of male children to Chinese parents, there has been a massive rise in the number of female babies being given up for adoption there. The government of China has sought to alleviate this problem by allowing Westerners to adopt. It can take on average two years for parents to be awarded custody of a child but the rules governing eligibility are more generous than those in the West (age of prospective parents not being seen as a major problem, for instance). Other developing countries also operate international adoption processes.

- **You can accept that you will not be a parent** and enjoy being an uncle, aunt or godparent and spending time with the children of friends and family.

If you feel desperately disappointed about not being able to conceive do think about seeking counselling advice to help you come to terms with it.

There'll undoubtedly be friends and aged relatives who can and will make ludicrous suggestions, such as standing on your head after sex, or eating raw eggs, milk and bull sperm for breakfast, to help with conception. Most of these will be of no help at all.

IVF – a user's guide

There are several main reasons why IVF might be right for you.

YOUR SPERM CAN'T DO ITS JOB

If this is the case you can have your sperm artificially inserted into your partner's cervix or uterus via a syringe, thus helping it to save the energy that would otherwise be spent swimming. It also helps avoid that nasty vaginal acid.

YOUR SPERM COUNT IS SO LOW IT COULDN'T IMPREGNATE EVEN THE MOST WILLING OF EGGS

Then sperm donation may be the answer. Specialist fertility clinics take and preserve sperm from anonymous donors (all of whom are carefully vetted). Information on the hair, skin and eye colour of the donor, as well their blood group, is documented to ensure as close a match to your own as possible. Donated sperm is given every possible check for health and vitality. The donor himself is also checked for communicable diseases or infections.

Although donor sperm is frozen and around half of it is lost in this way, the remaining half is guaranteed full-strength sperm. The same method of insemination is used as would be if it were your own semen. All information regarding the donor is destroyed after use. Of course sperm donation is a big subject, and something you both need to think about carefully, and discuss with specialists.

YOUR PARTNER HAS BLOCKED OR TWISTED FALLOPIAN TUBES

Her gynaecologist could unblock them or straighten them out without damage. It is also possible that she could have her fertile eggs removed from her ovaries, fertilized using your sperm (in a test tube) and then reinserted in her uterus for the normal term of pregnancy. The test tube fertilization period takes around three or four days. Often up to three fertilized eggs are reinserted in the uterus, increasing the chance that at least one egg will successfully grow into a baby. Which is why IVF treatment can sometimes lead to multiple births. Hey, at least you got your whole family in one go!

YOUR PARTNER CAN'T PRODUCE FERTILE EGGS

She could accept a donor's eggs. These have been donated by anonymous, healthy mothers who have usually given birth to healthy children previously. The collection procedure is more complicated and difficult than it is for donated sperm, of course, and the IVF treatment carries a greater risk of failure.

You've done it!

Quite possibly it has taken more than a month for your partner to become pregnant. Most likely there have been a few false alarms along the way. Women always claim to know when they're pregnant, just like they know when you've been with another woman or are lying about how that lovely vase from her mother got broken. Which means that at least once before the following scenario will have taken place:

'I'm pregnant!' she announces as you come through the door, whisky in hand and champagne in the fridge.

'What?' you gasp, eyes, mouth and arms wide open. 'Are you sure? How do you know? Have you taken the test?'

'No,' she replies. 'I'll get one tomorrow and show you for sure, but I just *know*. I'm a woman. I know these things. And, as I was walking past the deli on the way home I had a sudden craving for artichokes in olive oil, anchovies and taramasalata.'

Next day, though, the result is negative and there is sadness in the air for a month.

There are, of course, some more reliable indicators.

The signs are there, it's looking likely and now it's time to see for sure with the pregnancy test kit. That's it! It's come up positive. You can see for yourself. You're pregnant!

Signs that she is pregnant before the test proves it

These are the most common (though some may be red herrings ...)

A missed period. But then, that can happen even if she's not pregnant.

Frequent visits to the toilet. At a week after conception, her bladder will begin moaning about all the extra work it's going to have to do.

Sleeping more than usual and feeling tired more often. A pregnant body creates a lot of progesterone, which is a sedative.

Changes in her senses of taste and smell. Often pregnant women say that they taste metal in their mouth while eating. What were once favourite foods can become inedible and she might start to crave something unusual.

Morning sickness (hers, not your drink-induced purging).

Increased sensitivity of the breasts, making them painful to touch. Get used to it.

HOW TO REACT ON HEARING THE NEWS

With unalloyed joy and happiness. If you can, you should cry now. With her. Hugs, kisses, even intimate contact is fine and allowed. A glass or two of champagne is permissible, as is rich and expensive food. You are as happy as she is and will remain so for the foreseeable future. You should agree with everything she says (even if you don't, you can discuss it later) and give her absolutely no reason to think that you are not as happy as you could possibly be about being a dad.

ON NO ACCOUNT ...

Tell anyone else at this stage. Not your family, or hers. Do not tell your best friend, and make sure she doesn't tell hers. You can tell the cat or dog, because they can't talk, but do not tell any other person until after 12 weeks of pregnancy and the first scan, which shows how well the baby is developing. Those first 12 weeks of life are very difficult for an embryo and all manner of things can go wrong with the pregnancy. Telling people before this time creates a level of expectancy among friends and family that can adversely affect you both. You also get 12 weeks to share your secret and get used to how you really feel about it.

You may find this kind of dinner option being offered. Banana or anchovy? Sorry, banana and anchovy.

2 In the beginning

NOW THAT YOU'RE GOING TO BE A DAD THERE IS A WHOLE NEW WORLD OF EXPERIENCES TO BE HAD. A LOT OF THEM INVOLVE HOSPITALS AND DOCTORS, AND SOME OF THEM INVOLVE SHOPPING. THEN THERE ARE THE PROSPECTIVE GRANDPARENTS . . .

A testing time

You'll really know that you're going to be a dad when you've seen it for yourself. Which will happen about 16 weeks after conception when you can sit in the room and watch your partner have an ultrasound scan. It's not painful or messy – unless you count some gunk on her stomach.

THE ULTRASOUND SCAN

The nurse (or doctor) runs a small pad attached to a tube over the spot where your baby will be lying in the womb. Next to the trolley on which your partner is lying will be a television screen showing something that looks like the Milky Way as seen through a

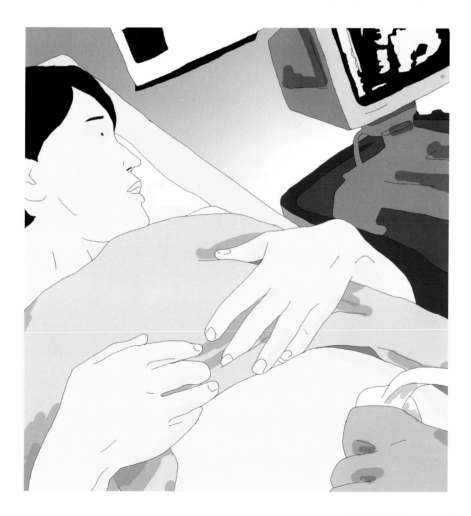

Special tests

If the doctors have reason to think that there might be a potential problem with your partner's pregnancy they may suggest performing a special test. These can range from a relatively painless blood test to a more invasive sampling of the placenta or amniotic fluid.

The most common reason for any test other than the usual antenatal ones at this early stage is the age of the mother. Because of the increased risk of the baby being born with a disability such as Down's Syndrome or sickle cell disease to a mother who is over the age of 30, a series of increasingly invasive tests are suggested.

THE ULTRASOUND

This is the first test, and it's the most straightforward test. It examines the baby's neck – an unusual thickness at the 16th week can indicate possible Down's Syndrome. This ultrascan method is often employed at the 16-week scan as a matter of routine.

THE TRIPLE TEST

In this test, a sample of the mother's blood is checked for unusually high levels of oestriol, human chorionic gonadotrophin and alpha-fetoprotein. Again, this test helps anticipate the likelihood of the child being born with Down's Syndrome.

This rather indistinct shape is what the first image of your child will look like – it's an ultrascan.

AMNIOCENTESIS

This is usually suggested to mothers who are over the age of 35 and involves the withdrawal of amniotic fluid from the womb via a long, very thin, needled syringe. The 15-minute operation is performed using local anaesthetic and is painless for the mother. There is some argument as to whether the test causes any discomfort to the baby, but as it is generally done at 14 weeks or earlier, the risk is considered to be minimal. Examination of the amniotic fluid can show whether the baby is at risk of a variety of problems, including Down's Syndrome, chromosomal defects, metabolic disorders and whether it is getting enough oxygen. It can also tell you the sex of your baby if you wish to know.

CHORIONIC VILLUS SAMPLING (CVS)

This is an invasive test. It involves taking a sample of the placenta at between 10 and 12 weeks, before the amniotic sac has fully formed. It can be performed either in the same way as amniocentesis or via the cervical canal using a catheter. It can detect Down's Syndrome, sickle cell disease and so on, as well as determining the chances of the baby suffering from cystic fibrosis, haemophilia, Huntington's chorea or muscular dystrophy at the earliest stage. CVS is most often suggested to women with a family history of such disorders and results can be obtained within one to two days. It does carry the highest risk to the baby, though.

UMBILICAL VEIN SAMPLING (UVS)

This carries a similar threat to the baby as CVS because a needle is used to take blood from the umbilical cord, although this time outside the placenta. The sample is tested for the same things as with CVS but can also detect any infection in the baby (such as Rubella or herpes).

Although the above tests may be suggested to your partner, she is under no obligation to submit to any of them. Antenatal clinics will give you percentage chances of the likelihood of any of these problems developing, but how you treat those percentages is up to you. If you are ever in any doubt about whether to have a test, seek a second opinion.

dirty telescope. After a bit of moving the pad around, the nurse will point to some indeterminate shape on the screen and say, 'Look, there's the baby'. You'll peer hard and hopefully but will probably end up pretending that you see something. Your partner will actually be able to make out the shape of a baby and you'll both be very, very happy.

If you want, the nurse will print the image for you and you can take it home. After a couple of days spent staring at it you too will be able to make out the shape in among the dots and swirls, and recognize it as your child.

ANTENATAL CARE

It's a good idea for you to make as many trips to the antenatal clinic or parentcraft classes with your partner in these early stages as possible. For the first 28 of the 40-week term of pregnancy she'll attend once a month. Then it'll be every two weeks until the 36th week, when she'll have to go every week. You won't be expected to go every time, but for the first four or five visits you should be there. She'll need you. She's never done this before. It's kind of scary. You might be scared, too, but please, ask yourself why? No one is going to be prodding, weighing and taking your blood, are they? No. So pull yourself together and be strong, silent and supportive.

Antenatal care at this stage will involve your partner having her height, weight and shoe size taken (the shoe size can give an indication of her pelvic inlet and outlet and therefore whether she might have trouble giving birth naturally). She'll also give a blood sample to determine her blood type and whether she has any viral infection or communicable disease. A urine test will check on kidney function. Later urine samples will show her protein and sugar levels. Her blood pressure will also be checked. She might have an internal examination (which you shouldn't be present for), but that doesn't always happen at this stage of the proceedings.

Got to tell the world

The doctors have given the OK, and you'll probably want to shout the news from the rooftops. If you don't, perhaps you should go back to the 'Be Sure' section of this book (page 12) and do the mirror test again.

So, how to let everyone know? And who's first?

GRANDPARENTS

Of course they're first. Hopefully your relationship with both sets of prospective grandparents is good. It will need to be,

because they can be either a great help or a terrible hindrance. If you can talk to them like adults (that is, they consider you to be an adult) then do so. And do it in person if you possibly can, rather than on the telephone.

Ideally, tell both sets of prospective grandparents at the same time. A family meal is a good time and place to let them know. Get them all together at your place or, if it's too small, in a restaurant – at least no one can explode with fury in a public place, right? And if anyone is likely not to be happy

Try to smooth out any rivalry between each set of grandparents by including both in discussions about family matters that involve them either individually or collectively.

about the news, you've got the whole family together and you can all try to make them feel better.

You and your partner need to decide at the very outset whether or not you want the grandparents to become actively involved in helping to raise your children – will they want to be used as babysitters or a child day-care facility, for instance. Try to smooth out any rivalry between each set of grandparents by including both in discussions about family matters that involve them either individually or collectively.

Don't exclude them, as they have had far more practice at this game than you have. It might have been a long time ago, but some things don't change with time.

FRIENDS

Once you've told the family, then you can begin to let your friends know the happy news. As with the grandparents, you might want to tell them all at once, so have a party or a big night out together. Friends who already have children will prove to be most supportive and useful to you as a couple and individually (unless they're unhappy and wish that they'd never done it, in which case you should probably not invite them to the announcement party). Most of your friends will feel happy for you. Others, particularly childless couples who have been trying for a while, may find it more difficult. Tell them

separately, and at an earlier stage. They may need time alone to come to terms with the news. There may be tears, and not just of joy. Do not be angry at friends who blurt, 'It's not fair', and run from the room sobbing. And don't patronize them, either. Let them deal with it themselves, then just forget that it happened.

YOUR FRIENDS

There are certain stages in almost every man's life that are defined by key events. Being chosen for a first team signals the beginnings of a **Sporting** stage. Actually the sporting stage usually lasts the rest of your life, if at a slight remove as you get older. Losing your virginity signals the awakening of the **Stud** stage. Leaving home kicks off the **Man** stage (kind of). Getting married signifies the **Adult** stage. Now that you are to become a dad, another stage of your life is about to begin.

The thing about each stage and each key event is that they usually involve getting to know a new bunch of guys, making new friends. Some will remain friends, off and on, for a long time, even reaching new life stages at the same time as you do. Others will drift away, as you both find your lives taking different routes.

While you might find that you disagree with friends about sport, sex, politics, music or even cars and yet remain pals, you are about to discover that it's a different matter when it comes to dadhood. Friends that you've known for a long, long time might become strangers overnight. This is because they have taken the mirror test (page 11) and found that they are depressed by being called 'Dad'. Tell these friends last – by that time you'll know how you feel and you won't care too much about how they react. The only thing you can do is be yourself and seek companionship among those friends who are genuinely happy for you. Most of your happy pals may already be fathers and the others will be hoping to become dads as soon as possible, or they will have accepted the fact that fatherhood is not for them but without harbouring any bitterness and resentment towards you. You guys are going to be pals for a long time yet, even if you don't see as much of each other as you used to.

HER FRIENDS

If you think you might have trouble with your friends, just wait until she starts telling hers. You might recall that time when one or more of her best pals approached you at your wedding (or at any time after she'd said that you were 'the one' to them) and sweetly threatened to castrate you if you ever cheated on her? Well, now they are likely to threaten far, far worse for any minor indiscretions on your part that make the love of your life and their best friend unhappy.

Her friends are more likely to suffer from jealousy and envy than yours. Your partner will be emotionally affected by it and you will have to offer her support without condemning her friends for being insensitive. Both will deal with it in their own way and the mother of your child will have a lot of other stuff to think about soon enough.

WORK

Putting an announcement on the staff noticeboard is not a good idea. Neither is emailing everyone with the news. Be cool. Tell your boss and let him or her know when you'll be expecting to take your paternity leave – and you will take it. Then let workmates that matter know in a low-key manner. If any are close friends outside of work and you've already told them before you have had a chance to tell your boss, ask them to keep schtumm until you can. If you are letting family and friends know over a weekend then either tell your boss first thing Monday morning or as soon as you can see him or her in private.

Don't ask for a raise or extra time off (other than paternity leave). Don't expect a cigar or staff party. Be prepared with all the relevant information, such as when the baby's due, whether it was planned, if you'll be moving house – the boss will be guessing your intention to either get a better-paid job or expect more money and a better position from the company. It's natural, your priorities are not your boss's priorities.

You should be thinking about these things anyway.

What can go wrong

Breaking the news to family can be quite a delicate operation, and can throw up some unexpected reactions. So be aware of the potential difficulties, be as prepared as you can, and be patient.

GRANDPARENTS GO APE

There's a chance that one or more of the expectant grandparents are not going to welcome the news. It could be that they simply don't like the idea of being called Gran or Grandpa (so don't, it's not funny). Or it could be that they think they will be expected to be unpaid nannies, supply childcare whenever asked, or are scared of handling babies after all this time.

GRANDPARENTS WANT TO BE TOO INVOLVED

If you're lucky enough to have an expectant grandparent who can't wait until the birth, it's a good idea to start as you mean to go on. Because they've been parents for so long and you've never done it before, some grandparents will insist that you do everything their way from the moment of announcing the good news. You have to rebel NOW. Do not let them become the masters of your pregnancy. Point out how modern healthcare and research have meant that so many things have changed since their day. Above all, make sure your partner is with you on this. After all, she'll be the one at the centre of all the focus and she'll have to say 'No' to them more often than you do. So support her.

GRANDPARENTS WANT TO MOVE IN

It happens. The partner may feel more comfortable with her mother around. As long as this is clearly a temporary arrangement, it might be OK. If your mother-in-law hates you and starts excluding you from everything, then you have to do something about it. Issuing an ultimatum that it's her or you will not work (you'll lose either way). Instead, try to get your partner to see what's happening in a non-accusatory way and enlist the help of friends and family who can support

you. Get your father-in-law to talk to his wife (if he's still around, of course). If they both want to move in then maybe you could live at their place ...

FRIENDS STOP CALLING

It happens. Sometimes men with no children of their own or who are separated from their family can't handle it. You have to let them go. Equally, there might be friends of your partner who are too jealous and envious to deal with it. Let them go.

AN OLD GIRLFRIEND STARTS CALLING

Some women seem to get off on the idea that an old flame is about to become a father to another woman's child when he wasn't interested in having children with her. This woman may reappear and want to have sex with you. If you do then she will make sure that the mother of your unborn child knows about it. (On the other hand, this just might be a big male fantasy, so don't worry about it.)

AN OLD BOYFRIEND STARTS CALLING

Not yours, hers. He could just be calling to offer congratulations to you both. He could be smugly laughing at you, the fool who fell for her tricks and is now trapped. He could still be in love with her and desperate to make her love him again because his ego can't stand it that he's not the father. Either way, if the old boyfriend calls, act nice. You're safe in your relationship and

nothing can change that. Unless your old girlfriend calls ...

YOUR BOSS FIRES YOU

There had better be a damned good reason for that to happen, otherwise you can sue them. If you're fired after announcing that you're having a baby, the company had better be either going out of business, massively re-structuring or have proof that you deserve it. Consult your lawyer.

YOU'VE CHANGED YOUR MIND

Tough. Get over it and enjoy.

SHE'S CHANGED HER MIND

She won't. She might have doubts and misgivings, but you'll make sure that they all disappear. Unless her old boyfriend calls ...

YOU WAKE UP

It might have been a dream this time, but it will happen. Oh yes, it will.

Do not let them become the masters of your pregnancy.

Building a nest

If you think that having a baby isn't going to make any difference to your lifestyle, then you are sadly mistaken. No matter how much you might want to carry on having Tuesday night poker sessions with the guys at your place – with all that cigar smoke, drinking and cussing going on – you can't. Not when baby arrives and not even while you're waiting for baby to arrive. A pregnant woman does not like a bunch of men smoking, drinking and swearing in her home while she's lying on her back with her feet in the air watching her waistband expand. Neither will she like it much if you come home from somebody else's house on a Tuesday night smelling of cigars, booze and swear-words. You might well find yourself sleeping on the ponyskin Le Corbusier lounger. If it's still there when you get back, of course. In fact, now you mention it, that white leather low-level Scandinavian sofa can go, too. And can't you get some carpets? Floorboards are so cold.

> ## A pregnant woman does not like a bunch of men smoking, drinking and swearing in her home while she's lying on her back with her feet in the air watching her waistband expand.

You see, even before your lifestyle changes, your immediate surroundings are likely to alter radically. The woman in your life is changing physically and emotionally and she is going to want her home to change too.

IS IT BIG ENOUGH?

Hey, that was in Chapter 1! Ah well, if you didn't get round to sorting out this one when you were planning your future finances, you'd better get on with it now. So, is it? Are there at least two bedrooms in your home? If not, do you have a sofabed in your living room? Because you'll need it, and soon. First you'll have family members staying over when the baby's born. Probably her mother, at least, will be there for a couple of weeks to help out. Then there's your mother. After that you'll be sleeping on the sofa in order to get some rest before going to work – the baby will be in your bedroom for at least three months and probably longer. If someone's sleeping in your living room, you are going to have to want the kitchen to be separate and not open-plan, aren't you. Or your house guests will have to be the first to rise in the morning.

And do remember to wear pyjama bottoms in bed when Grandma's sleeping on your sofa.

ARE YOU GOING TO MOVE HOUSE?

If you don't have enough space (or if your landlord doesn't allow children) and you want to move to a new place, you should get things under way as fast as possible. A remarkably high percentage of new parents choose to move home on discovering that there's to be a third person about the place.

Moving house with baby in mind

Ideally you should be installed in your new home a couple of months before baby is due. While you will have your reasons to move to any particular area, you should consider the baby's reasons, i.e. how close it is to the hospital or clinic where baby is going to be born.

If you're smart enough to start planning the move at the same time that you're planning to get pregnant, you will have chosen your antenatal clinic because of its proximity to the area in which you hope to live. (Yes, I know, if only moving house were that predictable – but you have to try!)

You should also consider how close it is to your partner's place of work. She'll probably be working up to and into the 7th month of pregnancy and she really isn't going to want to have to trek too far there and back again every day.

It's probably too soon to be considering the local educational opportunities for your child – unless you plan to be there for more than 5 years. Even if you do intend to stay at the new place for a considerable length of time, detailed investigation of school performances and reputations isn't necessary at this stage. Things change and you've got plenty of other matters to think about.

Make sure that you can afford to move to your ideal home. There may be only one income in your family for a while.

SETTING UP A NEW HOME

No matter how long you two have lived together, the arrival of a baby will change things. Physically, your home is about to undergo a makeover dictated by the mother of the unborn child.

- **Comfort** This is going to be highest on her list of priorities. You'll need a good, big, firm bed for the three of you (it's not going to be just you two for a while yet). You'll need a sofa that you can snuggle on (all three of you). A soft rug for baby to lie and then roll on would be good. More cushions and throws will also come in very handy.

- **Security** This is suddenly going to become a big issue for your partner. She is going to want to know that the neighbourhood is safe to walk around with a pushchair and not fear attack or kidnap. She's also going to want strong, double locks on all the doors and windows. It might seem bizarre to you, but she's protecting her baby. Think of Ripley in *Alien2*. So, even if you don't move house, you may have to invest in some new locks.

- **The nursery** Baby is going to need a bedroom. Despite not needing or being able to sleep in it for months and months. Preparing a nursery somehow helps focus

your thoughts on the fact that there is
soon to be another living being sharing
your home. It's kind of like preparing a
room in your old digs in order to get
another housemate in. Except with a baby
there's no rent coming in. And the decor's
likely to be more childish (although ...).
And in that bedroom there will be the
various items of furniture listed below.
You may also want to put a small sofabed
in too, so that you can use the room for
adults to sleep in.

STUFF FOR BABY

This is where you are really going to need
help. The chances are that you have not
previously shopped for a newborn. So you
don't know what you need. You'll want a
pram, a car seat and something for baby to
sleep in, you think. Which is correct. But
there's more ...

BABY WILL NEED

- A rush **'Moses' basket** (below) in which
  to sleep in your bedroom. These come
  with a simple wooden collapsible stand.
  The basket should have a fully fitted
  sleeping bag with pop-stud openings.

- At least three **all-in-one sleeping suits**,

which should be bought before baby is
born (get white), a coat, mittens and hat if
it's to be a winter birth.

- A **pram** rather than a pushchair. Newborn
  babies have to lie flat and be fully
  supported by the pram. The pushchair
  will come later. Actually lots of them will
  come later, they tend to wear out fast.

- A **car seat**. There are many to choose from and some manage to be all things at once – a car seat, a carrying basket, a pram and a time machine. OK, maybe not the last one.

BABY'S BEDROOM WILL NEED

- A **crib** with a **mobile** hanging over it (this should be suspended at a height that makes it impossible for the baby to grab it).

- A **chest of drawers** at hip-height (your hip) on which to change baby's nappy.

- Some **soft toys** – far too many in fact.

- A **soft nightlight.**

- An **easy chair** in which a parent can sit and gaze silently at their sleeping baby. You'll want to do it, believe me.

BABY'S BATHROOM WILL NEED

- A **plastic baby bathtub** that can fit into your bath, or be used on a flat, hip-height chest of drawers.

- A soft, enveloping **bath towel** or six.

- A **washcloth** that can be fitted like a glove on your hand.

- Somewhere to store **nappies** and **wet-wipes.**

STUFF FOR MUM

Whatever she wants and you can afford, give her. You've already got the sofa, bed and big items fixed. Here follows some other important stuff.

- **The right colour scheme** If your old place was dark and masculine, she's going to want things a bit brighter. But not stark white; this is not a hospital. Discuss and compromise to get what you are both happy with. Except in the nursery, where you won't have any say over the decor.

- **A footstool** As the pregnancy progresses she is going to want to literally put her feet up more and more. So get a matching footstool to go with the comfy sofa.

- **A clean bathroom**, preferably with a bath in it. Showers are OK, but a pregnant woman (and then mum with baby and even dad with baby) loves to soak in a tub.

- **Pampering** Rub her feet and shoulders when she asks. Pay for beauty treatments if you can manage it.

- **Maternity clothes** Most of these enormous gowns and expanding pants are horrendous. However, a careful search should unearth some shops that sell items that look like they're meant to be stylish rather than functional. You must always go shopping for these clothes with her, though. While pregnant your partner's brain will be a bit mushy and her taste might be a bit off. It's not permanent and hopefully she'll recognize the fact, thus allowing you to help her choose her clothes.

- **Constant reassuring** Tell your partner you love her at least once a day and sound like you mean it. Tell her she looks gorgeous (and she will).

STUFF FOR YOU

You'll learn to love all the new stuff. The new home, furniture and decor. But you might need a few things yourself in order to assist the difficult passage from unencumbered male to dad.

- **A space** There will be times when the mother and baby who share your home with you might seem not to know you exist. This isn't the case and won't last. However, you should have somewhere you can retreat to, listen to your music (use headphones), watch your movies or sport or surf the web and pretend that you're OK about it. After a bit of relaxed sulking on your own you'll be ready to get back into the swing of fatherhood.

Get a blender – smoothies for you, dinners for them and a good way to drown out those tantrums!

- **A still or video camera** on which to capture the early days of your child's life.

- **A good blender** Both you and your partner are going to need all the vitamins and minerals that you can get and there's no better or fun way to get them than in a fruit smoothie. Plus, the noise of it will drown out the baby's crying.

- **A clean suit of clothes and underwear** kept somewhere other than your bedroom in case you need to dress or change while mother and baby are sleeping. The nursery is the best bet.

- **A portable radio** Some experts claim that listening to static, or white noise, helps babies to sleep. So tune into nothing, put it next to the baby and see if it works.

- **The phone number of a good counsellor** Men often find it hard to deal with their emotions in the first couple of years after their child is born and it's good to talk.

In case you were wondering – the baby is …

… having fun in the womb, most of the time. As long as everything is fine with the mother, who is healthy, relaxed and enjoying herself, so is the baby.

Just because you can't see the baby doesn't mean you can't have fun with her, though. The baby can hear in there, so talk (and sing) to her. Not from across the room, up close. Rub your partner's tummy and talk straight at her belly button. Many experts believe that a baby can recognize its father's voice fairly early in life because it can remember hearing it while in the womb.

GIVING BABY A FUN TIME IN THE WOMB

- **Play music to baby** Apparently it can make him or her a genius. The classical pianist Glenn Gould, widely recognized as one of the world's greatest ever interpreters of Bach, started hearing his mother play while in her womb and for the first few months of his life would sit happily on her lap as she played the piano. Pretty much any genre of music will do – except thrash metal, gangsta rap or banging techno, obviously (if only on the grounds of taste). It would help if the mother liked the music too, of course.

- **Dance with baby** Gently. Swaying in time to music is very pleasing for your baby in the womb.

- **Take baby to the movies** As long as the films are not violent or scary and mum enjoys them too. It's thought that emotions are transmitted to the unborn child from

Ten soul songs to play to baby

'Rock Your Baby'
George McCrae
'Rock n Roll Baby'
The Stylistics
'Save the Children'
Marvin Gaye
'Baby Love'
The Supremes
'When Something Is Wrong with My Baby'
Charlie Rich
'Can't Get Enough of Your Love Babe'
Barry White
'Are You Lonely for Me Baby'
Al Green
'Maybe Your Baby'
Stevie Wonder
'Can't Forget About You, Baby'
Jerry Butler
'I Wanna Be Around'
James Brown

The baby can hear in there, so talk (and sing) to her.

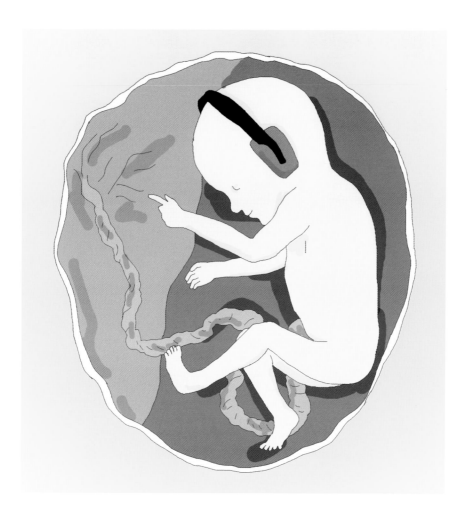

the mother. So a happy-sad movie will be a nice experience. For you, too.

- **Tickle the baby** Gently. Making mum laugh sends happy thrills to the baby.

- **Take baby's photograph** Take an image of the bump every month and then frame them with the final image of the newborn baby. In a few years your child will love it.

- **Eat chocolate with baby** OK, with mum. Chocolate is full of the amino acid phenyl-alanine, which is made in bundles by the brain when you're in love. Of course your partner's making loads of it naturally, but sharing a bar of 70% cocoa chocolate is one of those intimate, fun things guaranteed to make everyone happy.

Is it a boy or is it a girl?

Do you want to know what sex your child is before it's born? Why? If it's a matter of lineage and a title being handed down the male line, fair enough. I can't think of any other reason. Just because you can is no proper argument. Desperately wanting a child of one sex or the other is not healthy, or normal. Men who want only boys should ask themselves why. Would having a girl be such an insult to your machismo? If you think that you are capable of having only boy children then you are not just mistaken but dumb, too.

AND THE MORAL OF THE STORY IS …
When you think about the sex of your children, do you think about you first and them second? Your desire to have one sex over the other is saying more about you and your prejudices than anything else. You should know by now that nothing can be foretold. You can hope and dream but reality has a way of making fun of your dreams. It isn't better to have a boy than a girl, nor the other way around. And there are no statistics to show that one sex is going to have a better

It's a boy!

Assume that you are about to become father to a boy. Here are some good things that you can do with a son.

Play sports with him

Go to the game together

Buy a slot car racing game and play with him

Dress him in cool boy clothes

Name him after your father/grandfather/uncle/brother

Teach him how to drive

Here are some not so good things about doing all that with a son.

He might beat you at the sport before he's a teenager

He might not want to go to the game

He might prefer to play X-Box

He might prefer pink trousers

Every time you call him you think about your father/grandfather/uncle/brother

He could be stealing cars before he can legally drive

It's a girl!

Assume that you are about to become father to a girl. Here are some good things that you can do with a daughter.

Play sports with her
Go to the cinema with her
Buy lots of books to read with her
Dress her in cool clothes
Name her after your mother/grandmother/aunt/sister
Teach her how to drive

Here are some not so good things about doing all that with a daughter.

She might beat you at the sport
She might want to see chickflicks
She might want to read Barbie stories and not sci-fi
She might think that your taste in clothes is sad
Every time you call her you think about your mother/grandmother/aunt/sister
Her boyfriend could teach her to drive before she's legally able to

life than the other. Girls do better at school than boys but boys suffer less from eating disorders and bullying. Girls get pregnant but boys commit suicide. At least, unhappy ones do. Whether you have a boy or a girl is not the point. The point is that they know that you, their father, loves them unconditionally. Being told that they should have been a boy or a girl will damage them and make them unhappy. If it happened to you then you should know this. If it didn't, be glad. And enjoy your baby when it arrives.

Whether you have a boy or a girl is not the point. The point is that they know that you, their father, loves them unconditionally.

You name this chip (off the old block)

You have probably thought about what you are going to name your baby. If you haven't discussed it with your partner yet, then this is the time. You probably won't come up with a firm decision straight away but you might get a shortlist together. You should know, however, that many parents have a sudden blinding sense of inspiration at the moment the baby is born, and all previous ideas go out the window because as soon as they see him they just know he has to be Lancelot. Or Tarquin. Or that she has to be Britney.

KEEP IT IN THE FAMILY

There is a long and illustrious history of men naming sons after themselves. Kings and minor royalty did so in order to ensure the title would stay in the family. Businessmen do the same because their ego is on a par with that of a king. Some absent-minded fathers do so because they can barely remember their own name. The ex-world champion heavyweight boxer George Foreman named all of his seven children George. Even the girls. Go figure.

Women, being less egotistical than men, show less of an urge to follow this silly practice, though they may well wish to name their children after their mother or grandmothers. And that's something to consider. A lot of new parents take grandparents' and even great-grandparents' names for their offspring. The more diplomatic choice is to use both sets of grandparents' names (so George Albert, for example, or Mary Rose) so that no one can moan about it later.

Please note, however, that naming your son Junior with a number after his name, or your daughter little miss whatever her mother is called can only make you look like an egotistical idiot. And you really should investigate the possibility that the 'interesting' grandparent, great-grandparent or distant relative who holds a place of awe in the bosom of your family has a dreadful secret past. You never know.

Remember that Moon Unit Zappa, Zowie Bowie and Yeahman Stoker ... all changed their names to something very ordinary as soon as they were able to walk and talk.

The rules of naming

DO

AVOID THE EXOTIC

If you are in any way inclined to name your child after an exotic flower, obscure country, animal or insect, then please hold that inclination in check until you've done some research. First, examine closely the origins of the name – why is that Amazonian plant you like so much known colloquially among the Indians as the bloodsucker? Next, try out the name for yourself. When meeting strangers, introduce yourself with that odd name and gauge the reaction. Do they look sorry for you? Do they laugh out loud? Then ask yourself if you want to put your baby through that for the rest of its life.

BE SOBER

Do not decide upon your child's name when under the influence of any kind of drugs. Remember that Moon Unit Zappa, Zowie Bowie and Yeahman Stoker (son of the drummer of legendary psychedelic rock band Golden Bough) all changed their names to something very ordinary as soon as they were able to walk and talk. Their fathers were, of course, Frank, David and The Right Honourable Lionel. You might think it would be cute to be calling your child in the playground by the name of an obscure Eastern European beer or South American hallucinogenic plant but it's not. It's cruel.

BE INSPIRED

Choosing a name from literature, art or music is fine, as long as it's not ridiculous. So no Dracula, Salvador or Prince, right? Or Sherlock, Pablo (unless you are Spanish) or Beenie Man. Often the names of literary figures or authors are quite ordinary and so your child will not have to memorize a lucid and plausible defence of their name from the age of five or so. Calling your daughter O or Lolita is also completely out of the question, and if you were even considering it, are you fit to be a parent? Likewise calling your son Paddington or Frankenstein is cruel and stupid. Unless your surname happens to be Bear or Monster. You can call your son Louie if the song gets you going that much – but upon no account is he to be named Louie-Louie. You get the idea.

DO NOT

ATTEMPT TO BE MYTHICAL OR TOPICAL

Naming your child after a Greek god, character from a sci-fi novel or video game is a definite no-no. You should also resist the temptation to honour your favourite TV character, pop star or sports star by bestowing their moniker on your child. Your seemingly all-consuming adoration for that character/star will wane and in time you will not be able to call your child by their name without embarrassment at how dumb you were back then. Reality TV show contestants are the ultimate no-no. They hang around C-class openings for too long and end up in their own drug/sex/food bingeing hell. Is that how you want to think of your child?

GIVE YOUR SON A SEXUALLY AMBIVALENT NAME

Thankfully, the use of Hillary, Marion and Dana for men has fallen out of favour. Long may it stay that way. Consider the best intentions of the late, great Johnny Cash – calling your son Sue will not build character in him or make him tough and it might make him attempt to shoot you dead when he's old enough. Using what is traditionally considered a man's name for your daughter, however, could be good for her. Frances easily becomes Frankie, and she got the best of Johnny, remember. Lesley, Danielle and Sydney can easily be shortened to the apparently masculine Les, Danny and Syd. Employing such a name in business could be good for her since the world still regards men as being the dominant sex. The fools.

ATTEMPT TO CREATE A UNIQUE NAME

Ask yourself, would you like to be met with a bewildered stare every time you give your name and asked, 'Is that one X or three?' Creating a name for your child that is derived from your car licence or favourite ball player's

initials can only lead to bad things. Likewise, using a hyphen to join together two seemingly unsuitable first names is to be avoided. This is usually a device employed by hillbillies with too many teeth who share too many close-relation genes and is intended to signal to the two closest possible matches for paternity that the mother knows, and so will the child. In the event of it being a girl with two perfectly functioning first names hyphenated together, that would suggest that the mother or father of the child is not sure about the provenance of their own mother. Don't go there.

USE A BIZARRE SPELLING

Any attempt to make your child feel 'special' by spelling their name in an incorrect manner will only lead to embarrassment. Their friends and teachers will believe that you cannot spell and will simply feel sorry for the child. Employing a double 'ee' in a name where there should be either 'ey' or 'eigh' demonstrates a possible over-dependency on the use of phone texting in parents. And the use of punctuation where there should be a vowel is to be frowned upon (it is Natasha, not N'Tasha and Lionel, not L'nel). If your offspring are to be pop performers in later life they can chuck their own punctuation and odd spellings into their name when the time comes.

Favourite names

IN THE UK

The most popular names, according to the National Statistics Office in 2003, were:

GIRLS (previous year's position in brackets)		
1	Emily	(1)
2	Ellie	(4)
3	Chloe	(1)
4	Jessica	(3)
5	Sophie	(5)
6	Megan	(6)
7	Lucy	(8)
8	Olivia	(10)
9	Charlotte	(7)
10	Hannah	(9)

BOYS (previous year's position in brackets)		
1	Jack	(1)
2	Joshua	(2)
3	Thomas	(3)
4	James	(4)
5	Daniel	(5)
6	Oliver	(10)
7	Benjamin	(6)
8	Samuel	(8)
9	William	(7)
10	Joseph	(9)

Number of names derived from African-American singers in the top 50: 1 – Ella (No. 12)

Number of names derived from flowers in the top 50: 4 – Lily (No. 24), Jasmine (No. 30), Daisy (No. 31), Poppy (No. 43)

Diana has not been in the top 100 most popular names for the past 5 years.

Number of names derived from movie stars in the top 50: 1 – Harrison (No. 47)

Number of names inspired by the royal family in the top 50: 2 – William (No. 9), Harry (No. 11)

Number of names derived from Elvis in the top 50: 1 – Aaron (No. 43).

... would you like to be met with a bewildered stare every time you give your name and asked, 'Is that one X or three?'

IN THE US

The most popular names, according to the Social Security Administration in 2003, were:

GIRLS (previous year's position in brackets)			BOYS (previous year's position in brackets)		
1	Emily	(1)	**1**	Jacob	(1)
2	Emma	(4)	**2**	Michael	(2)
3	Madison	(2)	**3**	Joshua	(3)
4	Hannah	(3)	**4**	Mathew	(4)
5	Olivia	(10)	**5**	Andrew	(7)
6	Abigail	(7)	**6**	Joseph	(6)
7	Alexis	(5)	**7**	Ethan	(5)
8	Ashley	(6)	**8**	Daniel	(9)
9	Elizabeth	(11)	**9**	Christopher	(8)
10	Samantha	(9)	**10**	Anthony	(12)

Number of names that use a hyphen in the top 50: 0

Number of names that use bizarre spelling or incorrect punctuation in the top 50: 0

Number of sexually ambivalent names in the top 50: 1 – Sydney (No. 25)

Number of names derived from exotic flowers in the top 50: 0

Number of totally made-up names in the top 50: 0

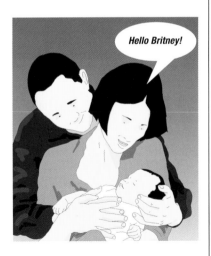

Hello Britney!

Take a break

After all the excitement of the past few weeks, what with finding out that you're pregnant and moving house, you'll probably be feeling a bit tired and emotional by now. So take a break. Being pregnant isn't a debilitating condition and there's no reason to think you can't jet off somewhere like you did before. Neither does being pregnant require specialist equipment (unless your partner has a specific condition, in which case, holiday at home).

WHEN TO GO

If you are thinking of jetting off to warmer, foreign climes in order to really get away from it all, then you should go before the sixth month of your partner's pregnancy. Although airlines will allow a woman who is seven months pregnant to board an international flight (although some put a limit at 26 weeks), by that time she is not going to be at all comfortable in a typical cramped airplane seat. It's not just the lack of leg room, the seat-belt restraints on her belly and the pressurized cabin that could play havoc with her blood pressure, it's the tedium of a long flight, the terrible food and the annoyance at having a bunch of strangers in such close proximity staring at her enormous stomach, nervous that she might give birth there in the aisle and that they'll have to hold fresh towels and hot water or something.

If you do take an international flight of more than an hour, make sure that your partner walks around at least once every hour – it helps with her circulation. In fact, why don't you follow her example.

WHERE TO GO

If you fancy somewhere hot, then you must first consider how the heat is going to affect your partner. She might have come to terms with her naturally beautiful pregnant state by the time you get poolside or on the beach, but is she really going to be happy wearing a bathing suit in front of all those strangers?

If you're heading for the sun aim for a place with a private pool or outside access that allows you privacy. Be prepared for your partner to take afternoon siestas – she's possibly doing that at home by the time you take a break anyway, but the extra heat is going to make her feel even more like having

Where not to go

Anywhere that has wild animals and no electricity

War-torn third world states

Anywhere where bandits like to kidnap rich Western tourists

Anywhere where you need to take malaria tablets

Ski resorts

Campsites (another general rule for life)

Golf resorts

Mountain-climbing centres

Anywhere that requires a flight of more than seven hours

Being pregnant isn't a debilitating condition and there's no reason to think you can't jet off somewhere like you did before.

a snooze. You may have a favourite holiday destination, one that you have visited together before and promised you would visit again. Well, now is the time.

Try to choose somewhere that will be able to cater for your partner's food cravings. It's also a good idea to choose a place where you're not likely to get an upset stomach because of the different local diet. If practical, carry food items that she might crave with you – as long as it's in a jar or can it should be fine – and make sure that the place you are travelling to will allow this. Do not carry fresh meat in your suitcase. That's a good rule for life in general.

Lastly, go for somewhere quiet and relaxed. You might have enjoyed holidays as a singleton at places where the clubs closed at dawn and you'd sleep until mid-afternoon, but that's no longer what you want from a holiday. A resort full of hard-partying people is not going to be the best place for a pregnant couple, trust me.

Things to take

The first thing to pack is this book, of course. You can swot up on what's going to happen as you lie on the beach or by the pool. It might make things a little easier for you to take in.

Travel insurance
Make sure it covers your partner while she is pregnant.

Familiar faces
Your parents or hers (or even both!) if you all get on well enough. This can provide an important feeling of security for your partner and a drinking buddy for you.

Friends
Good ones that won't mind if you guys don't want to party till the small hours.

Medical information
Check out the medical care centres and doctors local to your holiday destination before you leave and each take copies (in case one of you loses them).

Music
If the place where you're staying has a CD player, take your current favourite selection with you.

Check it out

We're about at the end of the first trimester here, so it's a good place to remind yourself about what we've covered so far. See page 237 for your results.

HELLO DAD
Take the mirror test (page 11).
Did you pass the mirror test? **Y** **N**

If your answer was No, go back and start again.

Are you sure? **Y** **N**

Is she sure? **Y** **N**

IT'S ALL IN THE PLANNING
Do you know what it costs to have a baby? **Y** **N**

Do you know where you will be living when you have a baby? **Y** **N**

Do you know where you'll be working when the baby arrives? **Y** **N**

TEST YOUR DAD POTENTIAL
(You'll find the results to your test on page 67).
Were you encouraged by your results? **Y** **N**

Were you scared by your answers? **Y** **N**

THE SCIENCE OF CONCEPTION
True or False The vas deferens is a new German luxury saloon car. **T** **F**

True or False A woman has two fallopian tubes. **T** **F**

True or False You know exactly where the fallopian tubes are. **T** **F**

HOW TO DO IT NATURALLY
True or False The chances of getting pregnant in the first month of trying are better than in the 18th month. **T** **F**

Ovulation occurs on day 7, day 14, day 21, day 28, whenever she says it does.

Is smoking big, clever and good for you? **Y** **N**

The optimum amount of alcohol that a woman should drink while attempting to conceive is 1 unit a day, I unit a week, whatever gets her drunk.

The optimum amount of alcohol that a man should drink while attempting to impregnate a woman is 21 units a day, 21 units a week, whatever gets him going.

Do you know where you can procure illegal drugs at 3 p.m. on a Saturday afternoon? **Y** **N**

True or False You are what you eat. **T** **F**

True or False Water's what fish live in. You wouldn't drink it. **T** **F**

HOW TO DO IT WITH HELP

True or False There's nothing wrong with your sperm. ☐T ☐F

True or False An ultrasound hurts. ☐T ☐F

True or False IVF always works. ☐T ☐F

YOU'VE DONE IT

Going to the toilet a lot can be a sign that a woman is pregnant. ☐Y ☐N

You are overjoyed at the news that you are about to become a dad. ☐Y ☐N

You can tell the world you're pregnant. ☐Y ☐N

A TESTING TIME

True or False Antenatal care isn't actually against anything. ☐T ☐F

True or False The triple test only happens once. ☐T ☐F

True or False Amniocentesis, CVS and UVS carry a small chance of harming the baby. ☐T ☐F

GOT TO TELL THE WORLD

You should telephone your partner's mother and call her granny. ☐Y ☐N

Friday nights with the guys at a lap-dancing club are history. ☐Y ☐N

WHAT CAN GO WRONG

Grandparents want to move in. ☐Y ☐N

Friends stop calling. ☐Y ☐N

You don't care. ☐Y ☐N

BUILDING A NEST

Minimal is out, comfort is in. ☐Y ☐N

You need at least two bedrooms in your home. ☐Y ☐N

You need to start thinking about what stuff the baby will need now. ☐Y ☐N

IN CASE YOU WERE WONDERING

Just because you can't see it this doesn't mean you can't talk to baby. ☐Y ☐N

True or False All geniuses listen to Bach while in their mother's womb. ☐T ☐F

IS IT A BOY OR IS IT A GIRL?

It doesn't matter. ☐Y ☐N

It really doesn't matter. ☐Y ☐N

YOU NAME THIS CHIP

You promise to think carefully about your baby's name. ☐Y ☐N

You will not make up a name, use a hyphen or take a pop star's name. ☐Y ☐N

TAKE A BREAK

You will start to plan a holiday as soon as the pregnancy is confirmed. ☐Y ☐N

You will go on holiday before the end of the second trimester. ☐Y ☐N

CHECK IT OUT

You will answer all of these questions truthfully. ☐Y ☐N

(Your partner will tell you if you answered correctly or not. She'll just know.)

'Test your dad potential' answers (see pp. 18–19)

YOU ANSWERED MOSTLY As

I don't believe you. What's with all that macho crap? Why are you reading this book? Get lost, creep.

YOU ANSWERED MOSTLY Bs

Not quite sure how you got past the mirror test. You're obviously deluding yourself that you are ready or even want to be a dad. If it's too late to stop now then you'd better change your ways. Hopefully this book will help. And lose the BMW.

YOU ANSWERED MOSTLY Cs

How are things in the armed forces these days? You like all those rules and regulations, huh? Well, you'd better start loosening up. Children do not like being ordered about and, if you're honest with yourself, you didn't much like it either when you were a kid. Get over it. Having children is not a duty or a right, it's a privilege and you know that you have to earn those.

YOU ANSWERED MOSTLY Ds

Are you sure that you're about to become a dad? I mean, it is your baby, right? It's just that you don't seem to have any kind of adult responses. Had a pretty sheltered life, huh? That's nice. But unrealistic. Sure it's great to hug your children but NOT ALL THE TIME. Get real.

YOU ANSWERED MOSTLY Es

You need a bit more perspective. You cannot always be there to protect your child. It might seem like your dad was always there for you when you were growing up, but that's the illusion he created for you – which is good. Speak to him and ask him how he managed to make you feel safe and secure and still have a life of his own. If he says that he didn't have a life, then that explains it.

YOU ANSWERED MOSTLY Fs

For once, scoring a big F does not mean failure. It's nice to know that there are some sensible people out there. It's not rocket science this stuff, is it? Hard work sometimes, yes. But you understand that and will probably turn out to be as good a dad as you can. Which is all anyone can ask.

What's going on?

IF YOU THOUGHT THAT WOMEN WERE MYSTERIOUS OR EVEN OTHER-
WORLDLY CREATURES BEFORE EXPERIENCING PREGNANCY, YOU ARE
ABOUT TO LEARN THAT THEY'RE POSITIVELY ALIEN.

What's going on with her body?

Pregnancy is calculated in weeks – 40 in total from the start of her last menstrual period (elephants have two years' gestation, so be thankful). When she finds out she's pregnant (that is two weeks since conception at mid-cycle) she's already technically four weeks pregnant (four weeks since her last menstrual period or LMP, as it's known in the maternity business). Confusingly, 40 weeks after LMP, the baby will be born – which is of course actually 38 weeks since conception. The hospital and antenatal clinic will keep referring to this date as the EDD, the estimated date of delivery. So, you can cancel any business trips you may have planned for the month around the EDD as soon as you know for sure.

Generally, pregnancy is divided into three trimesters. Each one consists of a three-month time period (told you this wasn't rocket science). You already know something of what goes on in the first trimester from Chapter 2.

- **First trimester** This is hell – and not just for her. She felt sick and premenstrual (it's the same hormones making her crazy as before she got pregnant). You'll have seen her loading up on carbs like biscuits all day, hating even the smell of coffee, aftershave, cooking and stuff. She's been falling asleep at 8.30 p.m. and every afternoon on the weekend. She takes a pee every 10 minutes and three times during the night. She has been grumpy, feeling vulnerable and emotional and her boobs are painful and hard as bullets. So don't touch them, or else.

- **Second trimester** This is a period of relative calm, you'll be glad to hear. The sickness has usually passed (at 12–14 weeks). Although she's getting bigger, at least she looks pregnant now, and not just fat (which really pisses her off). She sleeps, blooms, will have sex willingly, etc. Hopefully you're not too fond of your car, because she's going to scrape it against inanimate objects and walls, as her hand-eye coordination gets a bit wobbly …

- **Third trimester** This will be increasingly difficult as she gets bigger. She'll become more breathless and sleep-deprived (because she can only lie on her side), and will complain about looking like Rosie O'Donnell. If only. She will probably be frantically anxious about the birth: about losing control, the indignity of it (shitting herself, people shoving their hands up her like she's a prize heifer), the pain, that she or the baby will die. She'll worry about whether to take the drugs (yes, if necessary!) and about what she might say and do to you throughout the birth. That's just an early warning. More will come.

The pregnancy roller-coaster

Yes, you're in for a ride. Your partner will experience all sorts of things for the first time during the 9 months of her pregnancy, and you'll experience them with her. So it's best to be as prepared as possible.

HER PHYSICAL CHANGES DURING THE FIRST TRIMESTER (UP TO 14 WEEKS)

Her breasts will get bigger and harder very quickly after conception thanks to increased levels of oestrogen and progesterone. She'll go up a bra size quite quickly (and no, she shouldn't wear underwired bras during pregnancy). But don't go getting any ideas. They'll be too tender to touch.

The areola (the dark bit around the nipple) will become darker and bluish veins will be seen on her breasts as the blood supply increases.

Her metabolic rate will increase by 10 to 25% as her body (blood, heart, lungs, etc) works harder. Her blood volume increases by 25%.

Her breathing will become more rapid, and not just because she's happy to see you.

She'll need to pee more often, because her uterus is pressing on her bladder.

She'll want simple bland food – nothing spicy – so get used to it for a while. Some women get food cravings for soil, coal and other weird stuff, though it is rare and less likely if she eats well.

You don't need to be told this, but her moods will alter quickly due to hormonal changes. She'll be irritable, angry, frustrated, panicky, hypercritical, worried and unsure of herself. She'll probably share certain emotions with you at this time, such as her conflicting feelings. She'll resent being pregnant, but be thrilled by it at the same time. You do not have to say anything if she tells you this. Do not tell her that you feel the same way – it's not helpful.

She'll feel very, very tired, and need to sleep a lot.

Not many women are actually sick in the first trimester. It's called morning sickness because it is often worse then, but it can go on all day. Some women do vomit throughout their pregnancy.

Yup, there'll be weight gain: by the end of third month, she will have gained about 2 to 4lb around her middle and boobs. It might not sound like much, but she will feel big and swollen, which she'll hate.

Her libido will probably go down (though in some women it increases). Her genitals may appear darker and more purple in colour as the blood supply increases to that area.

If she normally gets spots before a period, they might break out now.

HER PHYSICAL CHANGES DURING THE SECOND TRIMESTER (UP TO 28 WEEKS)

Weight gain: she'll put on about 12lb during this period (1lb a week). Her waistline will disappear and she will look pregnant. She may get red stretch marks on tummy, boobs and thighs. You cannot see them.

Good news on her mood swings: she will feel more energetic and the sickness and tiredness will have passed.

Possible weird thing to happen: her nipples may secrete a milky substance called colostrum. You have been warned.

She may get constipated: pregnancy hormones relax muscles which means food passes more slowly through the gut.

Pardon: she may suffer from heartburn. The oesophagus relaxes and the uterus starts to push upwards against her ribs and stomach, which may cause some reflux, indigestion and heart pain.

She may start to sweat more because her body is working harder, and increased use of her thyroid gland increases perspiration.

Don't use her toothbrush: her gums may become spongy and bleed.

Backache: to compensate for an enlarged tummy, many women lean backwards, which causes backache. Of course she should avoid lifting.

The baby will start kicking, so she'll feel a fluttery sensation in her tummy. This is called quickening (it happens around 22 weeks, sometimes earlier).

Her hair will be thicker and shinier, her skin clearer. This is known as the bloom of pregnancy and is due to hormones.

You might spot a dark line that appears in the centre of her tummy and runs down to the pelvis. It's called the linea nigra and it fades after birth.

More good news: as her hormones balance out, she will feel calm, serene and positive. It gets better. Her libido will increase – some women have even been known to experience orgasm or multiple orgasm for the first time ever.

The pregnancy roller-coaster

HER PHYSICAL CHANGES DURING THE THIRD TRIMESTER (UP TO 40 WEEKS/BIRTH)

Weight gain: she'll put on about 10lb to the end of this period. She'll be getting bigger rapidly now and feel fat and unattractive. So keep telling her how gorgeous she is.

Don't try to walk anywhere fast with her. Walking will make her breathe more rapidly – which is a bit scary.

She will start sleeping badly – partly because the only way to sleep when you're this big is on your side with one leg up to your chest. It's hard to turn over. She'll be feeling tired again and so will sleep whenever she can. She may need to be propped up in bed to help with her breathlessness and heartburn.

Her backache will only get worse as her pelvic area softens in preparation for the birth.

Her ribs will feel painful as the baby pushes against them.

You'll notice that her navel inverts – and at last it can be cleaned out properly ...

Her skin might get itchy: don't let her scratch too much, but be gentle in stopping her!

She could start to get Braxton Hicks contractions, which are a kind of practice for birth. They're uterine contractions and last about 30 seconds.

Unfortunately (or not, depending on how you feel about it at this stage) her libido is likely to disappear again as she feels more physically uncomfortable.

She can't see her feet, so putting on tights or shoes is very difficult. So help her.

At about 36 weeks (though sometimes not until birth) the baby's head engages or drops down into the mother's pelvis. When it does, she'll start to feel more comfortable in the rib and chest area. Walking is going to be slow and cumbersome now, though.

She'll bump into things because her centre of gravity and eyeline are different in order to compensate for all that extra weight at front of her body. She might drop things, too.

This is a time of high anxiety. She will feel nervous about the birth. She might even be paralysed with worry – and will want to talk about it. She may be irritable, angry, frustrated and panicky, so be nice and don't argue or walk out on her.

This is her last chance to Nest. In the final few weeks of her pregnancy she may get the urge to clean the house – including the most ridiculously inaccessible cupboards and crannies that haven't been cleaned for years. Don't attempt to stop her, just accept that this is part of the deal, and offer to help.

… her moods will alter quickly due to hormonal changes. She'll be irritable, angry, frustrated, panicky, hypercritical, worried and unsure of herself.

Pregnancy ground rules

This is all new to both of you, but you are not going through any physical changes – unless you are enjoying a phantom, sympathetic pregnancy and piling on the pounds. For quite a while now and in the future, life in your home is going to be about her and the baby, so don't just get used to it – enjoy it.

Be nice Even when she's acting like a bitch from hell.

Reassure She needs to hear that it'll all be great and that you love her.

Be helpful Cook, clean, take her out when she feels like it.

Do not spend more time at work than is strictly necessary.

Do not attempt to hide from all that is going on.

Enjoy these days, because even if you have another baby after it, the first is always different.

Learn your lessons

You wouldn't jump out of an aeroplane without learning how to land, would you? It might seem different to you, but for the mother of your unborn child the prospect of having the baby is just as scary as that. Which is why she'll want to take various antenatal or parenting classes during her pregnancy. You should go with her, especially if she's asked you to.

ANTENATAL CLASSES
Antenatal or parentcraft classes are generally informal and take place at the home of the 'teacher'. There will usually be a course of

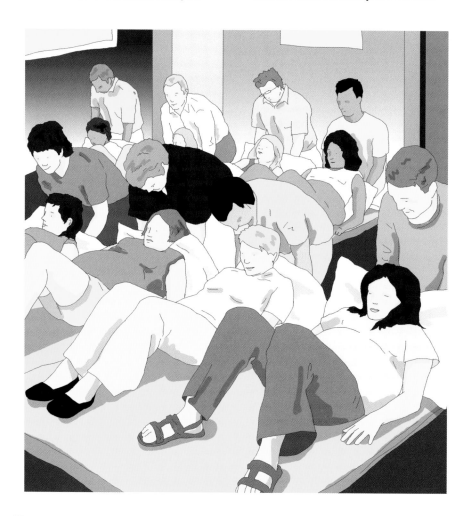

weekly classes involving a number of local pregnant couples. As well as providing you with a comforting approach to impending childbirth, the classes should offer you the chance to form an important (or so it seems at the time) network of local support among people who are all in the same state of anxiety and preparation.

A lot of the time in antenatal classes is spent talking about feelings. If you are uneasy about doing this with complete strangers try and relax so you can 'share' your hopes and fears for the baby with the others. You never know, you might enjoy it! If you really do feel uncomfortable about this then perhaps it may be best to not go at all. Maybe your partner will understand. You'll know.

As well as all the sitting on cushions swapping fears, there'll also be practical advice for both expectant mothers and fathers, so pay attention. You might get to view a video of a birth in full Technicolor gory detail. You will definitely be offered advice on how to assist your partner physically during the weeks leading up to and including the birth. You can learn breathing exercises together – and yes, she usually forgets about them as soon as the pain kicks in, so you'll have to remind her – and you will learn how to hold and support her as the birth progresses.

EXERCISE CLASSES

Giving birth uses muscles that you didn't know existed, and they could do with being built up before the big event. There are classes to help identify and then strengthen muscles relevant to different types of birth – water, standing, squatting, etc. These classes should also help with relaxation by offering advice on different techniques. You'll both need that.

TECHNIQUES OF CHILDBIRTH CLASSES

Pretty much what it says on the tin. These classes teach the mother how to dissociate herself from the pain by trying to focus on something else, and are reckoned to work well. Not always, of course. But by learning how to count to 20 before screaming again apparently helps to shorten the labour time. There are classes that teach her how to relax different sets of muscles, even under the stress of childbirth, and classes that teach a gradual tolerance of pain. These are all for her, not you.

YOGA AND STUFF

If you're lucky, you won't be asked to do yoga or Pilates with her. Unless you want to, of course. In which case, see page 100.

FATHER ANTENATAL CLASSES

Yup, there are dads-only antenatal classes available. Although not everywhere. Since they consist of men sitting around talking about their fears about what might happen during birth – in the reassuring presence of someone who can make them feel better, of course – you might think that a visit to a bar with a few pals is just as useful.

Change your life

As much as you might want to believe that having a baby is not going to change your life or lifestyle in any way, you are wrong. You might occasionally hear new parents claim that having little Jack or Emily has made no difference at all, but don't believe them. They are either lying or severely disillusioned. Just ask them if they always carried a shoulder bag, carry cot, car seat and squeaky toys around with them before the birth …

CHANGE YOUR MIND

This will happen gradually and naturally anyway, but to avoid any kind of shock to your system, consider this: the time that you now spend thinking about girls, cars, sport, beer or music is going to decrease. The time that you will spend thinking about the future, your financial security, how best to protect your family and about sleeping is going to increase. You are about to be redefined in the eyes of the world and people will see you in a different way. You will think differently about life from the way you did before you were a dad. For an idea of what this means find a recording of Frank Sinatra performing a song titled simply 'Soliloquy'. It's from the musical *Carousel*, and is written in the first person, the singer taking on the persona of a violent, wife-beating carny who's learned that he's

about to become a dad for the first time. (The birth of his child did not save his life, but it did save his soul, which is just as important in a musical.)

CHANGE YOUR CAR

Why not? You've wanted to for a while, right? So what better time than now, when you are thinking about safety, security and how to get a baby seat into a two-door, soft-top coupé. You can get a baby seat in the sports car, but you'll have to forget the mother of that baby, which probably isn't an option. Having a baby doesn't mean that you have to give up on cool or fast cars though. These days nearly all cars are safe – a good deal safer than when family cars had no seat belts, crash pillars or airbags.

CHANGE YOUR CLOTHES

For the first few months of their lives babies do little except eat, sleep, cry and vomit. They vomit after eating, but they also vomit whenever you hold them on your shoulder and gently pat them on the back. You might only want to wind the baby but it's rarely just wind that comes up. And it's not just when they're on your shoulder. It can be on your knee, in your arms or just lying next to you. When babies vomit you will get hit. So if you

You are about to be redefined in the eyes of the world

Family car basics

The model you choose should have all the following

A big trunk to take all the baby-related stuff that you'll be carrying around for months.

Parking sensors if possible, as the mother will still be having some trouble with her spatial awareness for a while after the birth.

As many safety features as possible.

Doors that clunk solidly when you close them.

A good stereo system.

Easy-to-clean seats.

Good acceleration, speed, handling, braking and looks. Doesn't every car?

RECOMMENDED FAMILY CARS:

Audi RS4

Most Subaru

BMW Tourers

Medium-sized SUVs

Mercedes Tourers

Sensible Fords

VW Passat Estate

TO BE AVOIDED:

Dodge Viper

Aston Martin Vantage

McLaren Mercedes

Big SUVs

Anything with two seats

Semi-Truck

must wear expensive shirts, trousers, suits or jackets you will have to accept the large dry-cleaning bills that come with it. It's a good idea to have a cloth that you put over your shoulder when holding the baby there, as it might catch some of the vomit. (But it'll never get all of it.)

So, why not buy some baby clothes for you? Buy stuff that is relatively easy to clean (machine-washable is best) and that doesn't show stains too readily, but in which you feel comfortable. You don't have to change your whole look just to cope with some baby sick, but you should think twice about winding the little kiddie when you're dressed for work in the morning. You'll find that trousers start to wear away at the knee after you've been a dad for a while. You'll be spending more time kneeling on the floor in the first few years, let alone months, of fatherhood than you ever did before.

CHANGE YOUR EATING

If both you and your partner are used to eating out a lot during the working week then the last trimester of pregnancy is where you're likely to see the biggest change in your eating habits. Weekend brunches with friends at bars, restaurants and each other's homes are going to be enjoyable up to and even after the birth, as long as the places that you meet are not too noisy, smoky or crowded. Spur-of-the-moment, midweek restaurant visits are going to become more rare, however, as your partner feels larger and more tired.

This is a good thing because it enables you to start cooking more. You can get adventurous in the kitchen as her cravings take strange shape. You can begin to develop a repertoire of 'signature' dishes. Pre-packed microwave meals will not be among them. Not only are they usually pretty dire-tasting and zapped of all their essential ingredients, but they cost too much.

CHANGE YOUR HABITS

The chances are that you have a few personal habits that are going to need to change before baby arrives. Sleeping until lunchtime at weekends is one. Friday-night drinks after work is another. Smoking is the worst of the lot. If you still smoke, you've probably already had quite a few arguments with your partner about it. It might seem as if you've all the time in the world to give up before the baby arrives, but you haven't. Feeling 'stressed' is not a good enough

Your partner is about to have a small, helpless human being totally reliant on her, needing her for 24 hours a day. The least you can do is help by keeping the rest of the house together.

reason to carry on with the nasty habit. It might be the toughest thing that you have to do before the birth, but you have to do it. There is no reason not to and every reason to stop smoking.

The use of recreational drugs is another unpleasant and childish habit that it's time to give up.

Refusing to do anything in the kitchen is a ridiculous habit, so lose it. Leaving your dirty laundry all over the floor, not changing the bedding regularly, never cleaning the bathroom and leaving the loo seat up are all habits that you have to break. Sure you've heard it all before and it's not directly to do with the baby, but it does all reflect an unconnected mind. Your partner is about to have a small, helpless human being totally reliant on her, needing her for 24 hours a day. The least you can do is help by keeping the rest of the house together.

CHANGE YOUR SOCIAL LIFE

Before pregnancy, and even up to the third trimester, you and your partner have probably enjoyed a pretty good social life. Meeting friends, going to clubs, gigs, theatre, the movies were all common activities. Are you worried that you're not going to be able to do all that any more? Well, you're not, but it's nothing to worry about. You'll spend so much of what was previously your leisure time with the baby – often doing other fun things – that you won't miss any of it.

And you don't have to completely give up on these things, just learn to do them in a different way.

Adapting your social life to baby

| Invite people to dinner or, better still, lunch, at your house instead of going out. Daytime eating dates allow friends to meet baby.

| If you haven't got cable or access to pay-per-view movies, now's the time to get it. Your living room can happily be your own cinema for a while.

| When the baby is old enough to be able to exist without the sight and smell of its mother, arrange for her to go out with friends one day a week while you babysit. Then you'll get a night out, too.

| Invite local bands to come and play in your living room. Then again ...

Huge and horny

You probably never thought that you would not want to make love with your partner. You also probably never thought about having sex with her at 6, 7, 8 or even 9 months pregnant. Now you have not only to think about it but do it, too.

FIRST POSITION

During the first trimester your sex life is going to be pretty much as it was, if a little more fun since you don't have to worry about contraception. Your favourite sexual positions and games can be much as they always were. Although you might find that she doesn't want to play naughty nurses any more. In which case you need to think differently. In general it's a good idea to be not too rough, too invasive or attempt deep

Six positions for sex with a large belly

1 Side by Side

With your partner lying on her back, you curled around and under her leg nearest to you. You'll build up your thigh muscles by having to hold your leg above and not on her hips.

2 Spoonful

She lies on her side with her back to you, her bum thrust out. You spoon around her. Or she lies on her side with her back to you, but straight. You lift her top leg and penetrate from behind. This stops penetration from going too deep.

3 Ride Him

An old favourite that's not affected by the size of her tum. You on your back, her on top, sitting up straight. It enables her to decide how deep is your love.

4 On the Edge

Of the bed. With her back on the bed (or table if that's comfy) and legs over the side, you stand or kneel as the height dictates. Hold her legs – she can move backwards if things get too uncomfortable.

5 Sitting Comfortably

You sit on a straight-backed chair, she lowers herself, with her back to you, on top of you. You can reach around, she can decide how comfortable to get.

6 Dinner for Two

Oral sex is easy and always satisfying, and there's no problem with her tum.

Pregnancy soundtrack

Ten recommended CDs you can listen to with the woman you love while she's pregnant

1 *A State of Wonder – The Complete Bach Goldberg Variations* by Glenn Gould (Sony Classical)

A 3-CD set of performances by the world's greatest ever piano interpreter of Bach.

2 *1* by the Beatles (Apple)

Babies love tunes. Honest. And what better tunes are there than Lennon and McCartney's number 1 hits?

3 *The Look of Love – The Burt Bacharach Collection* by Various Artists (WSM)

More great tunes, from the Carpenters' 'Close to You' through Aretha Franklin's 'I Say a Little Prayer' to Dusty Springfield's 'The Look of Love'.

4 *Music for the Mozart Effect: Relax and Unwind – Music for Deep Rest & Rejuvenation* by Various Artists (Philips)

The Academy of St Martin-in-the-Fields and the London Symphony Orchestra play some of Wolfgang Amadeus's most soothing piano, flute and horn concertos.

5 *Adventures Beyond the Ultraworld* by The Orb (Big Life/Island)

The album that began the whole Chill Out wave of recordings in 1994.

6 *Pop Pop* by Rickie Lee Jones (Geffen)

An album of songs from the golden age of the American songbook.

7 *Come Away with Me* by Norah Jones (Parlophone)

A younger Rickie Lee Jones, this is relaxing, cosy and laid-back. Perfect for wet afternoons on the couch for Mum and tum.

8 *The Very Best of Al Green* (Music Club)

A budget-priced collection of some of the best soul singing you'll hear from the very Reverend Green.

9 *Feeling Blue* by Paul Desmond (Camden)

The saxophonist's silky, smooth, almost soulful sound has great mellowness and warmth.

10 *Lemonjelly.ky* by Lemonjelly (Impotent Fury)

A ridiculously happy and bouncy recording, this is one to turn up loud and shout along with.

penetration. Not only can it be uncomfortable for her, but it might also upset the baby – and remember the theory that the child later remembers the voice and presence of adults who are close to their mother. Is that any way for your baby to recognize you? Not that the baby will come to any harm as a result of penetrative sex, it's surrounded by a strong protective sac and there is no way that a mere male member is going to damage it. Unless you've got twins or triplets on the way, of course. In which case your partner is unlikely to be able to move, let alone have sex, after three months.

SECOND POSITION

As long as the woman you love is enjoying a 'normal' pregnancy then you should enjoy a 'normal' sex life. It's common for pregnant women to feel a slight dip in their sex drive during the first three months, but after that their hormones are so up that they often turn into sex-mad mothers-to-be. And since they're sharing this wonderful experience with you, then you're going to be the lucky recipient of all that physical love she has to spare.

Of course there are also women who go off sex because of various physical (and emotional) reasons. The same swollen breasts and genitalia that she finds sexually stimulating can lead other women to feel uncomfortable. As former midwife and sex therapist Joy Peterson points out, 'Sex will be even better for some women and not as good for others. Increased blood flow to the pelvic area can cause engorgement of the genitals and heighten the sensation, but the same engorgement is known to give other women an uncomfortable feeling of fullness after intercourse ends. Also, some women may have abdominal cramps during or after intercourse. Her breasts, when enlarged, can be more tender, which can cause discomfort when they're fondled. She may also have more vaginal discharge or moistness which can make sex more pleasurable.' All of which means that either the woman you love will love sex while pregnant, or she won't. Which is not much different from not being pregnant for some of us, of course.

THIRD POSITION

And now the difficult bit, the bit that will upset some people. You, the man of the house, the reason why the woman you love is pregnant, may not want to have sex while she is pregnant, especially during the last trimester. Shocked? You will be when she advances on you at seven and a half months pregnant, belly first, tits of iron and horny as hell.

Since we men are supposed to want and be able to have sex with a woman no matter what state she's in, the idea of actively not wanting to have sex is considered ludicrous. Of course in reality it's less ludicrous than all those surveys which state that 70% of men have sex five times a week and affairs while only 33% of female respondents claim the same. Clearly those 33% of women are very busy with their affairs. However, despite not initially wanting to make love with her when she's in an advanced state of pregnancy, you cannot admit this. You can claim that you're worried about the baby, late for work/the game/haircut or something similar. You can claim a headache, exhaustion or beriberi, but you cannot admit that you do not find her sexually alluring. At the very least you have to cuddle. You never know, something might come up…

Strange days

Having a baby is one of the strangest things that you'll ever do. Since it's unlikely that you'll do it more than two to four times – statistically that is – then the experience remains an unusual one and the time you spend being expectant relatively short. Your first pregnancy will feel unforgettable in every way. During your second, you'll try hard to remember what happened the first time round. One thing's for sure: there are likely to be some very strange days. Most of them will arise from the mother of your child's seemingly irrational behaviour, but some will also be down to your own irrational actions. Here are some examples of what she might say and how you should react if she does.

- **She says that you don't love her** That no one can love her because she's so fat. However much you may know that this is ridiculous, it really is a test of emotional honesty for you. You have to say and keep on saying that you love her and then make her laugh.

- **She says your home is a mess and she can't possibly bring a child up here** There's every chance that you have just moved or decorated or had your home modified in preparation for the baby's arrival. No matter. This is your partner's fear and anxiety about her ability to be a good mother surfacing. It will pass. Meanwhile, seriously talk over any changes she wants to make and then 'sleep on it'.

- **She says you are working too much, staying at the office longer than normal** You have to ask yourself if this is true. During the final six weeks of the pregnancy, when it seems to you as if it's been going on forever and will never end, you may be working longer hours for a variety of reasons. It could be that you want to finish stuff before you take paternity leave. It could be an attempt to block the impending birth out of your mind, or it could be a bid to prevent her anxiety from affecting you (out of sight, out of mind? No way). None of these are good reasons to work longer hours. In fact, there is no reason to work longer hours, especially at this time. You should be getting home earlier.

- **She wakes up one morning and says she wants to take a few days away somewhere** So go. A change of scenery and routine could be good for both of you. Just make sure you're not going anywhere too remote or too far from home if it's in the latter stages of the pregnancy.

- **She announces that she wants to take up a different career** when the baby's old enough to be left with a carer. Having a baby is a huge life-changing event for a woman. It's having quite an effect on you, so try to imagine what it's like for her. Do not dismiss any idea she has, no matter how ludicrous it sounds. Talk it over and offer her support in whatever she wants to do. It may well never happen.

She loves you, yeah, yeah, yeah. She's just letting off steam. It'll happen. Don't take it personally.

- **There was nothing there when she looked but as she reversed she hit a wall/pillar/vehicle** It's only a car, the damage is not going to be that bad. You have to ask her how she is. You can probably straighten out the fender, wing or door easily enough.

- **She says you're having an affair** If she feels unattractive and her libido is low, she may worry that you are feeling sexually frustrated. You may be. She may accuse you of having an affair, or more likely to be thinking of having one. You won't be. You may flirt with someone at the office, in the coffee shop or with a close friend of your partner. But that's all you do, flirt. It never goes beyond a smile, a joke or two and a smile. There will be no physical contact or love letters, no intimate chats where you try to convince another woman that the baby's a mistake and you only agreed to have one for the sake of your relationship. Do not screw it all up now. Do not protest your innocence too strongly; do it honestly, quietly and with affection for your partner. Always look her straight in the eye.

How to be useful

You know there can be strange days, and you know that your partner is going through a wholly new experience that at times is making her confused and vulnerable. Your job is to reassure, and to be useful. Here's an easy-to-read, easy-to-follow list of dos and don'ts.

DO

BE THERE PHYSICALLY

Be with the mother of your unborn child as much as she wants you to be. Or be within easy reach. At the end of a telephone is not enough.

BE THERE EMOTIONALLY

Engage your feelings. Be scared, anxious, melancholy, excited, happy and sad. She is, and so should you be.

BE CONFIDENT

You might not feel as if you know what you're doing (you don't) but you have to be confident that you can learn and handle whatever it is that might come up. Your confidence should transmit itself to your partner, making her feel less anxious about your ability to handle what's about to happen.

BE QUIET

When she wants you to be. Noise can be as invasive as physical contact when it's not wanted. There will be times when she simply wants to lie on the sofa with a book or magazine and all you have to do is bring her hot drinks or treats.

TALK

To the baby. To the midwife. To the prospective grandparents. Most of all, talk to the mother of your child. Communicate.

SEE A COUNSELLOR

If you think it would help. The birth of a first child can bring about a wide range of differing and powerful emotions, which can be hard to understand and therefore handle. Getting into the habit of seeing an analyst before the birth can help you to continue seeing one after, when it may become more important.

BE HONEST

With yourself, and with your partner. If you are both honest with each other then your relationship can only improve.

COMPROMISE

Check the dictionary definition: 'a settlement of differences by mutual concession' (*Chambers English Dictionary*). The important word here is mutual.

GO TO CLASSES

If your partner wants you to, attend antenatal or parentcraft classes with her.

LEARN A FEW BASIC MASSAGE MOVES

Help to loosen her shoulders, feet and calves.

DRIVE

Whenever you're going places. She's stressed enough without having to worry about piloting a car. Plus, she's more likely to hit things when pregnant.

GET FIT

Now, before the baby is born. You'll appreciate any extra levels of fitness when you're being deprived of sleep and having to carry extra pounds around on your hip and in your arms (that's the baby we're talking about).

SCHEDULE

If you go to the gym or exercise regularly, or are going to, make sure that you do it on a schedule that your partner can plan her life around. Likewise, if you are going to have a regular night out without her (or she without you), try to keep it to the same night.

How to be useful

DON'T

PANIC

It'll be fine. You'll do perfectly well and possibly even brilliantly. Go to classes that can help you learn how to deal with things. Take up yoga, Alexander Technique or t'ai chi if necessary.

RUN AWAY

Being physically or emotionally absent during the pregnancy is only going to lead to big trouble for everyone – not least you. The mother of your child will resent your being absent, you will not build any kind of bond with the baby and you'll miss out on a unique formative experience.

THINK THAT YOU KNOW IT ALL

Because you don't. You'll never know it all. There will always be things that you have to ask about so don't be afraid to do so. This advice does not only apply to being a dad, of course, but to life in general.

ARGUE

Not with your partner, and not with family or friends if you can avoid it. Stress levels should be kept as low as possible during your partner's pregnancy (they'll already be high because of the impending birth). Any arguments you want to have with anyone that may impact upon your partner can wait. Then you'll probably have forgotten about it anyway.

GET ANGRY

If you do have to, do it somewhere else. Take up a sport or exercise regime that will let you work out any anger productively. You might get angry because of your partner's unreasonable and irrational behaviour, but you have to grow up and handle it. Remember that the baby can sense what's going on in its immediate surroundings. If it hears your voice yelling all the time, it'll be born with an inbuilt wariness of you.

Your friends, family and workmates will soon become bored by you if your impending fatherhood is the only thing you can talk or think about.

TAKE SIDES

In any kind of dispute between your partner and her parents. Try to see both sides of their argument (unless it's about you, in which case side with your partner of course) and ease any dispute to a non-conclusive end. If the argument hasn't been resolved when your partner has given birth and recovered, she'll be in a much better state of mind to deal with it.

INSIST ON SOCIALIZING ALL OF THE TIME

Your partner needs to rest a lot and socializing is incredibly tiring. If she wants to, then fine, but do not force it on her.

DRINK HEAVILY

Apart from the effect it will have on your health, heavy drinking will not go down well with your partner (she won't be doing it). It'll disrupt your sleeping patterns and you'll get enough of that when the baby arrives.

HAVE AN AFFAIR

Excuse me for stating the obvious – but see the book's title …

GO ON A SPENDING SPREE

You'll be tempted to buy lots of things for the baby, and for you, but you must resist. See the list of essential items to buy on pages 48–51. It's easy to get carried away in a baby store, but that's what they're designed for, so go only for what's essential. And ask yourself if you really need that new, huge TV, DVD or stereo right now.

BOOK AN EXTREME SPORTS HOLIDAY

Not even if you planned to go alone. There's always a chance that you will break something when skiing down a mountain on an ironing board, jumping out of a plane or kayaking down a fast-running river. This is not the time to put yourself out of action.

BE BORING

While it's important to prepare for fatherhood by reading the literature, taking classes and asking advice, it's almost as important to make sure that is not the only thing you do. Your friends, family and workmates will soon become bored by you if your impending fatherhood is the only thing you can talk or think about. Even your partner will want to spend some time doing, thinking and talking about other things.

Being useful around the home

KITCHEN

Shop for food, basic household goods and presents for your partner.

Cook whenever possible. And always ask her what she wants to eat.

Clean especially difficult areas, and everywhere during the third trimester. Even if you have a home help, clean. It will never be clean enough for your partner.

Wash dirty crockery and pans. Your clothes, and hers. Do the laundry regularly.

Put away Clean crockery and dishes, cleaning implements, anything that makes the place look messy.

BATHROOM

Clear away Do not leave wet towels on the floor. Clean any spills with anti-bacterial spray. Or when you miss the bowl.

Wipe up Keep the floor dry to avoid the risk of slipping.

Put down the toilet seat and lid when you've finished.

LIVING ROOM

Tidy Put cushions back on the sofa, take dirty cups or dishes away. Keep favourite music, DVDs and remote controls within easy reach of the sofa.

Decorate if it looks like a wood, steel and hard-edged bachelor pad. Go for comfort, warmth and carpets.

BEDROOM

Plump up Make the bed as comfortable as possible. Extra pillows will support her tummy and can be used to keep her legs high while sleeping.

Nest If your bedroom decor is minimal and white, make it softer. Make space by the side of the bed for baby's crib.

Chill out

As you are bound to have noticed by now, relaxation is a crucial part of the pregnancy. Stress levels need to be kept at a minimum for both the mother and you. Try to spend as much time together as you can and, when you do, try simply to do nothing. Of course, doing nothing is actually quite difficult. Luckily, there are plenty of other roads to relaxation.

EXERCISE

You might not immediately equate working up a sweat in a gym or running with chilling out, but it can be a great aid to relaxation and, more importantly, quality sleep. As for your partner, she will be shown a number of exercises that are proven to help with her preparation for birth at antenatal classes. These are some of the key ones.

THE FORWARD BEND

Feet must be a foot apart, flat on the ground and parallel. Hands clasped behind the back. Keeping the back straight, she leans forward from her hips. She holds the position and breathes deeply. When this becomes easily

achievable she can, while bent forward with hands clasped behind her back, attempt to raise those arms (with hands still clasped) up as far as she can.

THE PELVIC TUCK-IN

She kneels on all fours with knees a foot apart. She clenches her buttocks and tucks in her pelvis so that her back is arching upwards. She holds and relaxes without letting her back sink down again. To be repeated as often as feels comfortable.

THE LOWER BACK RELEASES

There are four main exercises designed to help strengthen your partner's lower back and thighs.

1 Lying flat with her arms by her side, palms down, she presses her feet to the floor and, breathing in, slowly lifts her pelvis so that her spine comes off the floor as far as the neck. As she breathes out she should lower her pelvis to the floor as slowly as possible.

2 Still flat on the floor, she brings her knees slowly up to her chest and hugs them,

taking deep breaths, all the time keeping her back straight and on the floor.

3 From the position above, she lets one leg straighten out and rest flat on the floor. After holding this leg for a few deep breaths she switches legs, hugging the other.

4 Again from the above position, she hugs both knees and crosses her ankles. With her arms flat on the floor (palms down) she slowly rotates her lower back in circles first one way and then the other, repeating as often as possible.

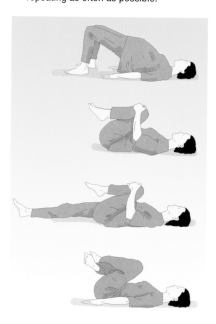

THE SPINAL TWISTS

Your partner lies flat on the floor with her arms spread wide, knees up and together, feet together and planted firmly on the floor. Slowly, she turns her knees either to the left or right and touches the ground with them, keeping ankles and feet together. As her knees turn one way, so her head should turn in the opposite direction (with arms still outstretched and flat on the ground). After holding for a few deep breaths, she turns her legs in the opposite direction and her head again in the opposite direction to that. Thus the spine gets a gentle twist, which aids suppleness.

These moves are good for you to use as warm-up and cool-down exercises, too. However, you should also be following your own separate exercise regime. If you had a regular gym or running schedule before the pregnancy then you should continue with it. You might even want to step it up a bit before baby arrives, because it might be difficult to keep to for a few months after the birth and there's no way that you can be too fit, is there?

SLEEP

Along with lower back pain, lack of sleep (or low-quality sleep) is perhaps one of the most common complaints among men and women in the Western world. On the arrival of your baby your sleep patterns are going to be constantly interrupted and you will both suffer sleep deprivation and its consequences. So it's a good idea to get in as much quality sleep now, before the birth, as you possibly can.

Our bodies need sleep to feel healthy and rejuvenated and that's why low-grade aches and pains are often felt on waking from a less than satisfactory night's sleep. Those aches can be made worse during the day and then hamper sleep the following night – and so it goes on, in a vicious circle that just makes for irritability and tetchiness. Of course if you're suffering from any physical pain that prevents you from sleeping you must seek professional help – a doctor or osteopath can help alleviate the pain via either drugs or physical manipulation of the painful area.

Prescribed sleeping pills can knock you out and aid sleep, but they can also produce adverse side-effects and in some instances be addictive. So first try one of the number of alternative medicines available that claim to aid sleep, or relaxation techniques. These will improve the quality of your sleep, making you feel refreshed when you wake rather than annoyed that morning is here already.

TIPS FOR BETTER SLEEPING

- Make sure your bed is **comfortable**. Not too hard nor too soft.

- Make sure your bedroom is **dark enough** and **quiet enough**.

- Only go to bed **when you are sleepy**. Don't toss and turn. Get up, go to another room and read or watch crap TV until you feel tired. Trying to force yourself to sleep when you're not ready will just make you feel annoyed and disturb the other person in your bed.

- Always rise in the morning **at the same time**, regardless of when you went to bed. That way your body gets into a sleep pattern (or at least that's the idea).

- Sleep only for **as long as you need to**. As you get older, lying in bed for too long can seriously disrupt your sleeping pattern.

Serotonin

It's what makes us happy and able to relax. Naturally created in the brain, serotonin helps the production of melatonin, which in turn helps us sleep properly. Stress and anxiety limit the production of serotonin and this can lead to depression and further suppression of natural serotonin production. If you want to be happy, keep your serotonin levels up! Exercise helps, as does laughing, eating chocolate and taking various supplements, such as 5-HTP, Vitamin B6 and St John's Wort (although St John's Wort should not be taken if you are on certain prescribed medicines. Check with your GP).

The stages

There are five recognized stages of sleep that occur regularly during a night.

1 Drifting away

The starting point, the one most difficult to crack for all insomnia sufferers (which an astounding number of people claim to be). As you drift off you may feel as if you're falling. Muscles can twitch. Waking up now will mean that you can at least recall your dreams, but you might be too scared to go back to sleep.

2 First real sleep

Once here, your eyes stop moving and your brain calms. Occasional fast brainwaves interrupt the slow ones. Less easy to wake from, but still disturbable by noise or movement.

3 On the abyss

Researchers into sleep patterns have recognized the creation of slow, delta brainwaves during this period. Smaller, faster waves intersperse the delta, but this is the precipice hanging over the period of deep sleep that you are about to fall into. More difficult to disturb.

4 The abyss (deep sleep)

Now you're sleeping. It's very hard to be wakened from this stage. Your eyes and muscles are almost paralysed and your brain is emitting only the slow, delta waves. If someone does wake you from here, you'll have no idea where you are or possibly even who you are.

5 Shiny, happy sleep (Rapid Eye Movement or REM dream sleep)

The final stage of sleep is the most active. As the name suggests, your eyes move a lot. However, despite your heart rate and blood pressure also increasing, arms and legs remain as if paralysed – which is why more people are not physically kicked out of bed during this phase. You are doing a lot of dreaming while in this state. Not that you're likely to recall much of it. Which is probably just as well.

Most sleep patterns follow a process of Stages 1, 2, 3, 4, 3, 2, 5 and back to 1 then repeat, with stage 5 (REM) becoming more drawn out as the night progresses.

- **Exercise** either in the **late afternoon** or **early evening** if you can. Exercising too late in the evening will over-stimulate you and prevent you from getting to sleep.

- **Avoid too much alcohol** before bed. You might drop off quickly, but you'll be woken by your body as it tries to expel the poisons from the alcohol during the night. That means several trips to the lavatory in the dead of the night, head banging and nausea rising.

- **Don't eat too late**, or too heavily, in the evening. A heavy meal takes time to digest and you're forcing your body to do that even while you want to be asleep.

- **Don't catch 40 winks** during the day if you can help it. Sleep at night, in your bed, when you are supposed to sleep. Not at your desk or under a table after a big lunch.

- **Don't go to bed mad**. You'll spend time fretting and thinking up the witty ripostes that you failed to think of during the argument that made you so mad. When you should be sleeping. Always make up, apologize or agree to disagree before attempting sleep.

DEALING WITH INSOMNIA

There are various causes of insomnia. Fortunately, the most common – stress – is also the easiest to deal with. Long-term insomniacs may be suffering from an illness (physical or psychological) that requires medical treatment, as a result of which sleep may be difficult to regulate. People who are unfortunate enough to suffer from this kind of

... lack of sleep (or low-quality sleep) is one of the most common complaints among men and women in the Western world.

insomnia need to treat the cause first. Often they are prescribed medication that merely deals with the symptoms. Unfortunately that medication can also prove addictive. Anyone suffering from medically or psychologically induced insomnia needs professional, medical treatment.

Stress can be caused by problems at work, at home, money and – you guessed it – even the impending birth of a first child. Most commonly this kind of insomnia is short-lived. In order to keep it as short-lived as possible, sufferers should identify the root cause (sometimes this alone is enough to aid sleep) and then work hard at chilling out (see above). Melatonin (the natural hormone that regulates sleep) is available in the US as a natural remedy, though it is only available on prescription in the UK, where it is most often replaced by 5-HTP. Natural health experts recommend taking mineral supplements of calcium and magnesium together every day. Nutritionists recommend eating a banana before bed (or anything small that is rich in carbohydrates).

The chill-out room

In an ideal world, your living room will have everything in it to help you both chill out. Getting it equipped now, before the baby arrives, is a wise move – everything will definitely be used once you have baby home with you.

SOFA
As plump as possible within the boundaries of taste. Have extra cushions available, a throw, too. There should be a footstool (for her, not you) close by so that she can put her feet up.

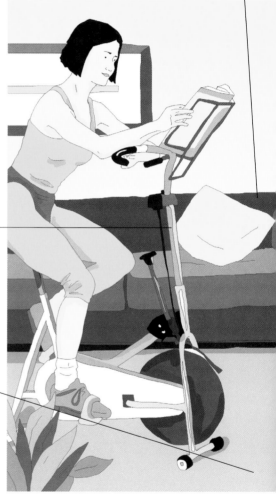

EXERCISE BIKE
Or a treadmill. It will help her to keep exercising for as long as possible, without having to go to the gym. You can use it during those long, sleepless nights ahead.

FLOOR SPACE
For either joint or solo yoga sessions, transcendental meditation (TM), Alexander Technique or massage – you don't want to have to move furniture around to make room to do the lotus or dog position. You might want to keep a yoga mat close to the designated floor space.

COFFEE TABLE (or side table)
She is not going to want to eat every meal in the kitchen as the pregnancy progresses, and putting plates and cups on the floor will invariably lead to irrevocably stained carpets.

BOOKSHELF (or shelves)
Keep all instructional books (like this one), novels, magazines and reference material here. That includes take-away menus.

FLOWERS
At least once a week, preferably twice, bring home fresh flowers and put them on the mantelpiece or a bookshelf.

VISUAL ENTERTAINMENT CENTRE
A widescreen TV with DVD or video player, cable or satellite connection (or at least a digital box!) is imperative. You can watch movies, sport and instructional videos together. Everything must have a remote-control box and be easy to operate. You might even want a games console wired up.

TELEPHONE
If it's cordless, keep the base here, so it's always to hand. If it has a lead and non-detachable handset, keep it close to the sofa.

AUDIO ENTERTAINMENT CENTRE
Keep all her favourite CDs close to the player. The stereo should be either on top of something high enough to be well out of reach of baby, or in a closet that can be locked. You'll appreciate it later.

Get in shape

In the previous section (pages 91–2) you read about the kind of exercises that the mother of your unborn child is doing to help her to prepare for the birth. You could and probably should be doing those with her, helping her to get through them where possible. However, that alone is not going to prepare you for the physical ordeal ahead.

THE BIRTH

While all the pain is going to be endured by your partner, you are going to have to be physically strong, too. Imagine that this is a secret mission. You must not crack under a lot of duress. You'll be asked to support a considerable weight at times – that of your partner as she goes through various physical positions in an attempt to ease her pain.

Why not save time and still exercise properly by swimming while at work?

- She'll stand facing you, leaning heavily on your shoulders.

- She'll half-squat as you hold her under the arms.

- You'll help to lift her from prone positions to standing and back again.

- You may be subjected to face-on abuse from her as her pain increases and it's all your fault. You do not complain.

Then there are the sights and smells you've never experienced before (unless you work in the medical profession). You will shut those out of your mind and nostrils.

AFTER THE BIRTH

If you've managed to establish a regular exercise routine prior to the arrival of the baby, then you should have attained a certain level of fitness. That will now gradually be eroded as you endure sleepless nights, a new level of stress and a bunch of new, difficult emotions. You won't be able to get to the gym as much as you did before. That's because your partner is going to need physical and emotional support from you pretty much constantly for the first few months (although that will lessen as you both discover that the baby won't break if left alone for a few minutes).

So you need to help yourself to stave off total physical collapse:

- **Exercise at home** Remember that exercise bike or treadmill you bought and put in the garage? It's still there and you can use it any time, even at 3.30 a.m. when you've just got baby to sleep again

but know you can't drop off straight away. Remember not to overdo it, though.

- **Run** Again, it can be done at any time as long as you have reflective running gear. You won't feel like it at 3.30 a.m., but you might three hours later. When you are back at work, if you can't always get to the gym, try running. Some men run to work and home again. Yes, I know they look stupid, it was just a suggestion.

- **Cycle** Like running, only you can go further, faster. If the stationary bike in the living room is too dull, get a real bike and use it to get to work and back. Even 20 minutes a day will make a difference to your level of fitness (and weight).

- **Use the baby as a training weight**

A different way to stay fit

For some reason, often the only man in any yoga or Pilates class is the teacher. And what about Alexander Technique, dance or even walking? Men don't do this stuff as a rule. But why not? Is it because we consider them to be feminine activities? Or could it be that we fear being surrounded by scores of women wearing leotards and tight tops? Yeah, right.

YOGA

Make sure you try a beginner's class first, otherwise both your pride and your body will suffer. It's not easy to do yoga and while you might think that it's not exciting or dynamic enough for you, you'll soon discover that it gives a different degree of fitness – and in different parts of your body – than any amount of running, skiing, throwing or catching. Improved balance, stronger muscles and new suppleness will make you feel better about yourself and help you sleep better. It might also improve your sexual stamina and performance. It's not guaranteed, though.

LIE BACK

If you're asking what TM, Alexander Technique or similar disciplines have to do with fitness then you don't know anything about them. They might not employ large muscle groups in dynamic activity but they help develop that most powerful and attractive muscle, the brain. (Please, no letters. I know it's not really a muscle, but I'm using the term metaphorically. Jeez.) Ignore the embarrassment of having to listen to this kind of hippie speak and listen when I tell you that each seeks to help you to find a calm space within yourself. Alexander Technique, which is usually

conducted one-on-one, aims to help you move and act in ways that reduce strain (and therefore stress) on your body.

WALK

Yep, simply putting one foot in front of the other is one of the best forms of exercise ever invented. And when you combine the physical act of walking with taking in the sights and smells of Mother Nature, you have a truly winning combination. Once the baby is born, you'll find yourself wearing a strappy sling type thing around your torso and a small human being clinging tightly to you within it. So get training now. Buy some good strong walking shoes or boots and when baby is born take him or her for a walk in a forest, field or over country terrain. Don't go anywhere that is dangerous or remote, obviously, and don't go out all day without the proper provisions. Start with half-hour strolls and then build up to longer hikes. You might find that you enjoy it so much that you start walking everywhere.

SWIM

A truly aerobic exercise, swimming is a great fitness-aiding activity. And babies love it. The earlier you can introduce baby to a pool the better. They'll never have a fear of water and will be swimming perfectly before they know to be scared of the stuff.

DANCE

An 'exercise' that you and your partner can certainly do together and have fun in the process. You probably won't be able to take the baby with you to evening classes, but you will definitely find yourself dancing or swaying with the baby in your arms at home at all times of the day or night. Dance classes will help build up your leg muscles so that you can sway the baby to sleep no matter how early in the morning it is. Plus, it'll do wonders for your sense of rhythm.

COOK

If you can't cook by now it's about time you learned. OK, it doesn't involve too much physical exertion – unless you're chopping the onions incorrectly – but at least you are standing up (and you know what you and your family are eating).

Take classes or buy books that tell you how to cook the simplest things, and practise every evening. Watch cookery programmes if you must, but be sure to take notes as you do. If your first attempts are terrible then you'll eat less and so have the motivation to improve. Cooking is not rocket science. It's incredibly rewarding, involving and good for you. You'll find that meals cooked by you are far better than those you get delivered to your door. You'll learn about what goes into each dish and with a bit of luck you'll start to take more of an interest in what you buy in the supermarket. Reading the lists of ingredients on tinned and ready-made foods can be a sobering experience.

The birth

AT LAST THE MOMENT HAS ARRIVED AND YOU HAD BETTER BE READY. AS WELL AS MAKING SURE THAT YOU CAN BE THERE FOR THE BIRTH, YOU ARE GOING TO NEED TO TAKE A LOT OF STUFF WITH YOU. WHICH IS JUST AS WELL, BECAUSE YOU'RE GOING TO BE CARRYING THIS STUFF AROUND FOR QUITE SOME TIME NOW.

Born free

For many couples, the question of where the baby is going to be born never arises. No doubt some people think it's illegal to have a baby born in your own home. No doubt others have never seen the inside of a hospital and wouldn't like to, either. Being male you'll most likely be in favour of hospital delivery; it's the sensible option. They have helpful machines, doctors and experience of delivering children successfully. At your place the machines either wash clothes or make coffee, there are no doctors and you only have experience of delivering newspapers. And that was a while ago.

AT HOME

As remarkable as it may sound, home births are safe. Although very much a minority activity, accounting for fewer than 10% of all births, those performed at home carry a much lower risk of complications. Women giving birth at home are less likely to need a Caesarean or forceps delivery. Home births do tend to be favoured by older women, the majority of whom are having their second, third or more child, but those that choose this method have only good things to say about it.

If you opt for a home birth, your GP might not agree with your wishes, of course. In which case, if you really do want to choose this method and there's no obvious risk in doing so, change your doctor (but note that both UK and US health authorities prefer the first child to be born in hospital). Your midwife will arrange antenatal deliveries at home and help you to prepare for the birth there. The major benefit of a home birth is that your partner will feel more comfortable than in the spartan surrounds of a hospital. You might think you'll need to replace the living room carpet as soon as possible, but that is of minor importance when weighed against her wishes. If she does insist on a home birth and it is possible, make sure she agrees to be taken to hospital in the case of any complications.

From your point of view, a birth at home will mean that you won't have to rush the expectant mother to the hospital in time for the birth. You might still have to rush through traffic, however, if you're trying to make it home from work. It also means that you can immediately retire to your own bed in your own home, rather than either sleeping in a chair at a hospital or having to make the journey home, alone, after the birth. And during labour you will both have the 'comfort' of being surrounded by familiar objects, furnishings and that lovely plush carpet. You can make as much tea or coffee as you wish. You can even watch TV.

IN HOSPITAL

You will have done your research into which is the best hospital a long time ago. There will have been several visits by both of you (but even more by her), so you'll have a certain level of familiarity with it. It's not home, but then, you decided against that.

There's no doubt that the hospital is the place to be if there are any problems with the birth. There will be a team of midwives, nurses and orderlies, all there to help out. Hopefully. Even the biggest hospitals get busy. The delivery room will have a supply of painkilling drugs on hand. You'll already have

It's in the blood

Just because your partner is opting for a home delivery that doesn't mean that she can't have a water birth. Neither does it mean that the bath has to act as the birthing pool. There are a number of companies that hire birthing pools out, so order one in plenty of time.

A water birth can ease your partner's labour pains by helping her to relax. There is little risk of the baby drowning, since he or she will immediately be lifted out of the water. This will be by either the mother, the midwife or a qualified water-birth attendant. Or even you. Plus, the baby continues to receive oxygen from the placenta via the umbilical cord for a few moments after the birth. People who claim to know about such things say that since a water birth is less traumatic for the mother it is less traumatic for the baby. Thus, goes the theory, baby will be happy and contented for the rest of its life. Which would be nice.

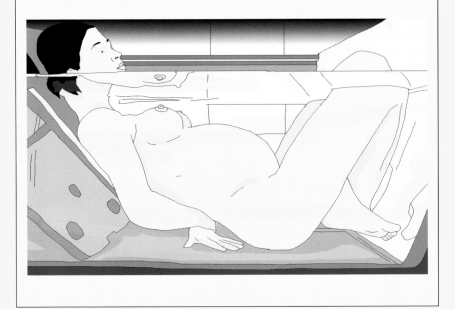

discussed the possible use of painkillers with your partner, and sensibly decided they should be used if the pain gets really bad. But if your partner is saying no to drugs, then you must back her up. If you've opted for a hospital water birth, there will be a big, solid tub (not the child's paddling-pool type that you could hire for home delivery).

The possible downsides of a hospital delivery are that there might not be anywhere for you to sleep, that the surroundings are functional rather than cosy and that the hospital is full. If an overnight stay is needed, during labour you can be present but if it looks like being a very long time, you may have to go home only to return in the morning.

Try to be completely aware of what is happening in the delivery room and make sure that the doctor and midwife include both of you in any discussions about the labour, especially if they are trying to force your partner into a Caesarean delivery. A very busy hospital may want to do this in order to free up the delivery room. That is not reason enough to suggest a Caesarean. Any argument for a Caesarean should be a very strong one, particularly since the baby can be more traumatized by this type of delivery than the mother. A sudden thrust into the glare of the operating room can shock the child in a way that a natural, vaginal birth does not.

There has been considerable concern in recent years that far too many women are opting for elective Caesarean deliveries for cosmetic reasons (it means that the vagina is not stretched) and it is estimated that in the UK one in five births are Caesarean.

Caesarean section

So named because the Roman emperor Julius Caesar is said to have been delivered via an opening in the womb rather than the natural way, the Caesarean section takes place in the operating theatre and normally lasts about an hour. Partners are usually allowed to be at the mother's bedside during the procedure. If the operation is an emergency procedure, however, the partner may not be allowed in the operating room. The most common medical reasons for a doctor to suggest a section are that the baby's head is too large for the mother's pelvic opening or that the baby is in the breech position (head up, see right). If it is lying across the mother's pelvis or the placenta is in the wrong part of the uterus (called placenta praevia), a section will lower the risk of complications during delivery. Diabetic mothers are also often advised to have a section. During the operation, the mother's abdomen is opened horizontally at the bikini line, followed by the uterus. The amniotic fluid is drained and the baby lifted out. The mother is usually under epidural anaesthetic.

On your marks

Now that you've decided where you want the birth to take place, you need to get everything ready. If you've chosen a hospital birth then you'll need to make sure that your route there is planned. If it's to be a home delivery, you'll need to make sure that your home is completely prepared.

THE CAR

If you're planning on driving to the hospital when the baby's on its way, make sure that the car is:

- **Available** Don't lend it to friends or family for at least a month around the birth date. Not even for an evening.

- **Working** If you don't use it very often, check daily that it runs. Start the engine or better still take it for a spin and get it to operating temperature.

- **Full** Keep at least half a tank of petrol in the car. If your journey needs more than that, keep it full. But you really shouldn't be trying to get a woman who is about to give birth to hospital in a 4.0-litre TVR or Lamborghini sports car.

- **Clean** Ensure seats are free from debris and detritus (no one wants to have to endure the stink of rotting fruit or vegetables, especially if they are in the early stages of labour) and make sure that there is no petrol can rolling around in the back. Whether empty or full, the fumes from them are sick-making.

- **Legal** It would be foolish, and potentially disastrous, to be stopped en route to the maternity wing because of a broken stop light, malfunctioning indicator, bald tyre or loud exhaust.

If you drive to work, make sure that you know the quickest route home or to the hospital at all times of the day.

Your availability

You will need to make sure that you can get to your partner and/or the hospital as quickly as possible if her labour begins during the day and you are at work. If you drive to work, make sure that you know the quickest route home or to the hospital at all times of the day. If you can take a cab, tell them why you're in a hurry. If you cycle to work, all the better. Just be careful in your hurry. If you've taken to running to work, forget about running home and get a cab. If you work in the city but live in the country or a train journey away, make sure that there is someone who can fill in for you with your partner until you get there. That friend, neighbour or family member who offered to drive her to the hospital should do. Make sure that you've agreed it before the time, though.

OTHER TRANSPORT

Hopefully you are not planning on using public transport to get you and your partner to the hospital in time. If you are, forget it. If you cannot drive or do not have a car, you have a number of options

- **Book a cab** Speak to your local cab firm and let them know that you may well need a car in a hurry around the estimated date of delivery. With luck they will be friendly and helpful enough to put a couple of cars on stand-by for you and be expecting the panic call.

- **Ask a neighbour** If there is a neighbour who is also a friend ask them if they'd be willing to provide the emergency transport to the hospital. Hopefully, they'll think it exciting and agree. If they do, make sure that all of the above comments hold true for their car too. And make sure that they are around during the day, as well as at night.

- **Ask a friend** If you hardly know your neighbours, ask a friend or a relative to be your driver. Preferably one that lives close to you. Or one that can stay over for a few nights until it happens. Again, check daytime availability. In a real emergency, ask the local shopkeeper.

- **Call an ambulance** Check local attendance times for the ambulance service. If it's satisfactory, you can depend on them. If it's not, choose an alternative from those above.

Get set

The route to the hospital is fixed and arranged. But it isn't just you and your partner that you need to get there. If you can have the following items packed and ready to go, maybe even already in the car, you'll find the whole procedure will go much more smoothly.

THE MOTHER'S BAG

There is a good chance that your partner will be spending a few hours or even a night or two at the hospital. So she'll need to take a bag of essential items with her

- **Nightdress** She may well be given a medical gown for the birth, or be naked, but as soon as she's in bed after the operation, she'll appreciate having her own nightwear. Pyjamas are not a good idea.

- **Night-bag** No matter that she'll have no thoughts of makeup or beauty products during or even immediately after the birth, she'll want to take some with her. A face cloth, her favourite soap and some perfume will also come in handy.

- **Childbirth book** There will be one book of advice about having a baby that your partner will favour over all the others. Make sure that you know which one it is and pack it for the hospital. She may never look at it, but it'll be reassuring to know that it's there.

- **Something to read** A novel or non-fiction title that your partner can read herself to sleep with, or pass what might be long, dull hours waiting during labour. Again, it may never be even opened, but no matter.

- **Favourite moisturizer** For her hands and face.

- **Favourite pillow**, or the pillow from her bed. It might not fit into the bag, so carry it separately. It'll help her to sleep.

THE BABY'S BAG

Yes, not even born yet but the baby has its own bag. What, did you think the hospital would give you clothes and essentials? Or did you envisage bringing it home in swaddling that would somehow magically appear in your arms?

- **Baby changing bag** No, not something in which you can take it to the maternity ward and swap it for one you like the look of more. It's a bag that comes with lots of pockets and a long strap and it contains all of the stuff you'll need for the nappy-changing operation. It'll be a permanent part of you and your partner's wardrobe for a while to come, so choose one that you like the look and feel of. A neutral colour is good.

- **Nappies** Get used to buying them, you'll be doing a lot of that in the months to come. The smallest size possible, of course. You won't need the whole pack, but six should do it (you're bound to wreck a couple putting them on at first).

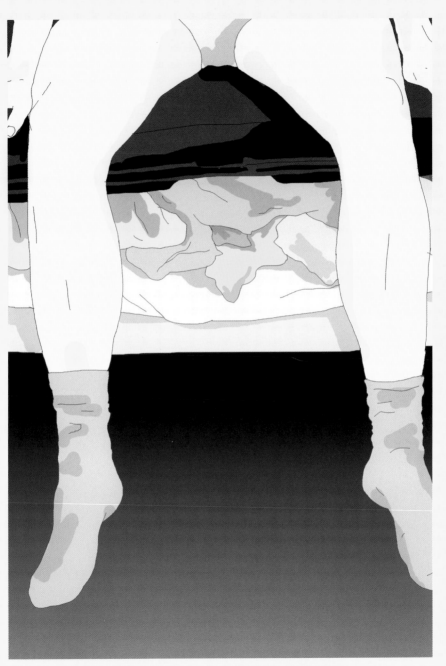

This is why you need to pack the overnight bag ready to go to the hospital in advance.

Now that is a well-ordered and prepared baby bag. Get one.

- **Sleep suit** Forget about the colour, buy white. They come in packs of more than one. They fasten at the crotch and are easy to get on a newborn. If your baby is due in the summer or late spring, get short-sleeved ones. If it's winter, go for full sleeves.

- **Sick blanket** Usually of muslin, they come in multipacks and are useful for keeping your clothes free of baby puke.

- **First toy** Something soft, colourful and that the baby cannot put in its mouth and swallow.

- **Baby blanket** These are always knitted with large open patterns. Not quite net-like, but not far off. That's so baby doesn't suffocate itself if the blanket – which you'll wrap tightly around your baby to make it feel secure – does get over its face.

- **Changing mat** Often they come as a detachable part of the baby's changing bag (see above). If you need a separate one, get something that can be folded small enough to fit into the bag and leave room for everything else.

- **Baby wipes** Wet tissues that can be used for a variety of things, but primarily to wipe baby's bottom.

- **Zinc cream** It'll help a lot with baby's sore bottom.

YOUR BAG

Actually, you can probably get it all in your pockets, so don't bother with a bag.

- **Spare car keys** In case you forget where the other set are.

- **A mobile phone** Switched off while in the hospital, but essential for keeping everyone up to date with progress and then to deliver the news of the birth.

- **Small change** Coins for the telephone if you don't want to leave the hospital, plus coins for the coffee or drinks machine.

- **Parking money** If you have to pay to park while in the hospital, make sure that you know how much it is likely to cost and that you have the funds (in the correct denominations) to cover it.

- **A camera** If your mobile phone can't take photographs, buy a small, disposable camera. Do not take photographs of the birth. Do take photographs of the mother and baby when the mother says that it is OK to do so.

- **A list of people** you must call after the birth, in the order that you will call them, with their numbers written clearly next to each name.

- **Proof of identity** So that when you are a gibbering wreck and unable to communicate who you are or what you are doing, usually when you arrive at the hospital for the first time, you can look at it and calm down.

Do not take photographs of the birth Do take photographs of the mother and baby when the mother says that it is OK to do so.

The miracle of birth

You know what's going to happen. You understand why it's happening, and why. But when it does happen to you, when you witness the birth of your first child (and any that may follow, too), you will believe that childbirth is a miracle.

IN THE DELIVERY ROOM

Your attention will be totally on your partner for the first hour or so, since you're expecting a baby to appear at any moment. This will not happen. After you've proved that you can help support her in the many positions that she'll be trying out to aid pain relief, you can start to look around. At least in between the contractions you can.

EARLY LABOUR TIPS

* Get to know the midwife by name – you'll probably forget it as soon as the

baby appears, but you'll have more success asking her for things if you know her name.

* Get to know how far it is to the emergency delivery room in case of any emergencies.

* Let the midwife and doctor both know that your partner has complete trust in you and that, if necessary, you will be making sure that she gets whatever she wants. Within reason – she may well call for your balls to be put through a sausage-maker at some point in the labour. You can ignore this and any similar requests.

* If you've asked for a water birth, check out the birthing pool. Don't get in it, but check the temperature of the water.

MID-LABOUR TIPS

* Make sure you've been practising the breathing techniques you learned at antenatal classes in the weeks leading up to the birth and keep demonstrating to your partner how to do them.

* Do not shout at your partner or in any way order your partner to do anything.

* Massage her back, feet, neck or anywhere that she asks.

* Make sure that the midwife is keeping track of your partner's cervical dilations at regular intervals. Your partner must resist

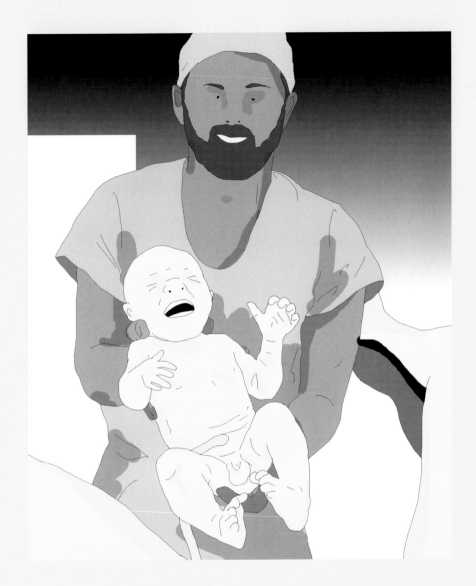

... when you witness the birth of your first child (and any that may follow, too), you will believe that childbirth is a miracle.

the urge to push until told that her cervix is ready.

DELIVERY TIPS

- If your partner has decided that she would like painkillers, back her up in her request to the doctor.

- Your partner should be in as upright a position as she feels comfortable with. This could mean that you are supporting her in some way – she could be leaning back against you, with your hands under her arms. If in the pool, she could be floating with your hands under her arms. She could be squatting, leaning on your knees as you sit on a chair in front of her. Be prepared to be a physical support.

- If you do not want to see the baby emerging – and you'll probably be asked by the midwife or doctor if you do – be strong enough to say 'No' if that's how you feel.

- If you are going to watch the baby emerge, do not make any involuntary noises that might be interpreted as shock.

- The baby takes about an hour to travel through the birthing canal and appear in the world. During this time you are going to feel as if you've pretty much been forgotten. You haven't, of course, and your constant presence, comforting words and physical support will be greatly appreciated.

Delivery room no-nos

Do not attempt to 'lighten the mood' by telling jokes or doing impersonations.

Do not use your mobile phone to call anyone.

Do not take photographs or video film until the birth is over. Unless you have the express, written agreement of the mother and hospital.

Do not faint. If you are in danger of doing so, leave the room and rest a while.

Do not shout at anyone. Remain calm at all times. Remember your TM or Alexander technique training.

Do not call the baby by a name before it is born and only use the name if you have both agreed before labour on what that name will be.

Do not get in the way of any of the professionals in the room.

Do not take notes. You'll remember all that you want to later.

Forget about the catcher's mitt, and do not rush round to try and intercept the baby as it emerges.

The first day of the rest of your life

How does it feel? Like the best thing in the world that you've never experienced. Nothing comes close. Do you remember the first time that you had sex, the first time that you won anything, the first drink you had? Well, it's not like that. It's better.

CRY

You will feel like it. You may even do it. Tears can easily well up and spill down even the hairiest cheek when your baby is born and you see it for the first time. Don't worry about it. Every man, or at least those smart enough, cry when witnessing the miracle of birth.

LAUGH

You'll be so happy that you won't know whether to laugh or cry. So you'll laugh. A lot. You'll laugh as the squashed-up, grubby, possibly hairy little thing that is your son or daughter lies on your partner's chest and squirms. You'll laugh as the nurses ask the baby's name and as you're asked if it's a boy or a girl.

WOBBLE

You'll feel weak. Your legs will be like jelly, your arms heavy and your head light. If the labour has been a long one then part of that might be because of lack of food. Most of it will be down to the fact that you've just realized that you no longer have only yourself to consider. That realization is enough to make you weak at the knees.

PANIC

Will you drop it? Will it break? How do you hold a small baby? When is someone going to come and take the baby away, because there's no way that you can be responsible for it? You'll be scared of everything for a while.

WONDER

Is that it? What next, where to, how long do mother and baby stay in hospital? You might even wonder who you are and why you are there. You certainly won't know what to do for the rest of the day.

Every man, or at least those smart enough, cry when witnessing the miracle of birth.

What to do

As you are feeling all that wealth of emotions, you will have some concrete things to take care of. After checking on the health of both mother and baby, the first thing you should do is hold your baby. Baby will be wrapped in either a hospital blanket or that nice new one that you remembered to bring with you. Nurses will have clamped the umbilical cord, cleaned baby up a bit and want to know what to put on the plastic name tag.

Check on mum

How is your partner? If she needs further medical care (stitches perhaps) make sure it's all done as quickly as possible. Tell her you love her and are proud of her (you are).

Check on baby

The nursing staff should have checked whether everything is functioning properly with your baby after the mother has had a bonding session. They will count fingers, check that all orifices are open and clear, that breathing and heartbeat are regular, that muscle tone is as expected, reflexes are normal and that the skin colour (which can signal a breathing problem) is correct.

Name that child

If you haven't decided yet, tell the nurses to tag her as baby whatever your or your partner's surname is.

Be alone with her

Both parents should be left alone with baby so that you can all get used to each other – it's just you guys now.

Talk to her

Your baby will 'remember' your voice from her womb. Hold her 10 inches from your face and she'll be able to see you – so smile – that impression of your face will stay with her.

Call

Get out that list you put in your pocket before leaving for the hospital. Either go outside the hospital premises to use your mobile phone, or go to the call phone with all that change you remembered to bring with you for this very purpose.

Take a walk

Mother and baby will want to sleep together for a while after the birth. You can sit and watch. Or you can take a walk in this brave new world. Everything will feel different, no matter how familiar the area. Even coffee will taste different, better.

Be there

Make sure that you are with mother and baby as much as they want you to be that first day. You'll be fetching and carrying, but you won't mind at all.

Say 'Hello Dad'

To yourself in the rest room mirror. How does it feel?

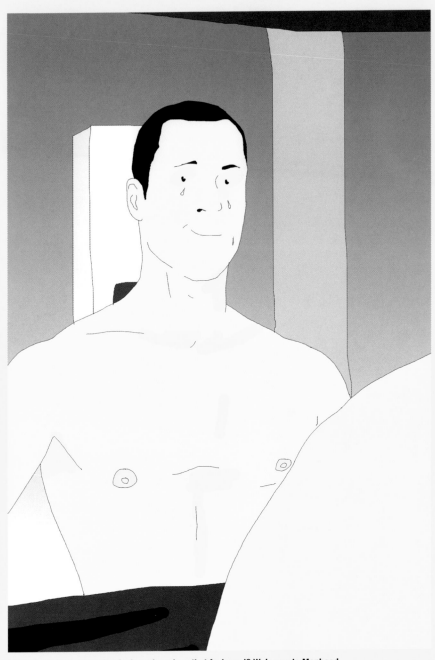

'Hello Dad!' Now, does that feel good, or does that feel good? Welcome to Manhood.

4 Hello Dad!

ONCE YOU'VE GOT BABY HOME, THE FUN BEGINS. YOU'LL SLOWLY
REALIZE THAT YOUR LIFE CAN NEVER BE THE SAME AS IT WAS AND THEN
YOU'LL BEGIN TO HAVE DIFFICULTY RECALLING WHAT LIFE WAS LIKE
BEFORE BABY ARRIVED. SLEEP BECOMES A PROBLEM FOR EVERYONE.
GRANDPARENTS NEED HANDLING SO THAT THEY DON'T BECOME A
HINDRANCE. THEN OF COURSE THERE'S THE MATTER OF HOW TO DEAL
WITH HAVING A GIRL CHILD . . .

Being there

Now you are three. A new way of life is beginning for everyone in your home. For the first two weeks at home the baby will need only its mother, and it will need her constantly. The mother will need you pretty much constantly too, to do the housework, to help keep her sane and to tell her how fantastically she is dealing with motherhood. It's all as strange to her as it is to you.

You will need to be at home for those first two weeks after the baby's birth – or after mother and baby's return from hospital.

PATERNITY LEAVE

If you are British it's going to come as a great relief to know that the law states that you are allowed two weeks of paid paternity leave. You are entitled to it even if you are not the biological father of the child, but are married to, or are the 'partner' of, a woman who has just given birth. If you are American your situation will vary depending on the particular state in which you live. There is no federal law in the US that specifically allows a father any paid leave to help care for a newborn; in the State of California, if your employer agrees, you can take up to six weeks' paternity leave on partial pay, but elsewhere the best that you can do is to take up to 12 weeks medical leave without pay. Of course the legal provision for paternity leave, and the maximum amount of time you are allowed to take are constantly changing.

ELIGIBILITY

In the UK you are eligible for paid paternity leave only if you:

- Have responsibility for rearing the child **OR**
- Are the mother's husband or partner **OR**
- Are the child's biological father **AND**
- Have worked continuously for your employer for a period of at least 26 weeks, that period ending with the 15th week prior to the child's birth

For the first two weeks at home the baby will need only its mother, and it will need her constantly.

CONDITIONS

At present in the UK the period of paternity leave has to be either a week or two weeks taken consecutively, not in daily increments, and must be taken within 56 days of the child's birth.

THE PAY

A father is entitled to £100 per week or 90% of his average weekly earnings if they are less than £100 per week.

THE EMPLOYER

You must tell your employer in advance what the EDD is and confirm whether you are taking one or two weeks. You'll also need to confirm when you want the leave to start (it could be a day or so before the EDD, or after). If you change your mind about when you want your leave to begin, you must tell your employer 28 days in advance of the start date – unless it is an emergency or it is unreasonable to expect you to do so.

PROTECTION

Employees are protected by law from unfair treatment or dismissal as a result of their wish to take paternity leave.

Maternity leave

IN THE UK

At present a woman is entitled to up to 26 weeks' paid maternity leave. During that time she will receive 90% of her normal pay for the first six weeks from her employer, and £100 per week for the remaining 20 weeks of the leave period. Or she will receive 90% of her earnings for the full 26 week period if her earnings are equivalent to less than £100 per week. Employers can claim 92% of payments that they make to a woman on maternity leave from the government. Small companies can claim 100%.

IN THE US

There is no law governing statutory maternity leave and no company is obliged to offer it. There are slightly different rules governing each state, so you should check to see which allowances are offered by the state in which you live, if any.

At home with baby

You may have felt that there were already three of you living at home for the past 3 months or so, but this is different. For many new parents, the overriding feeling during the first few days spent with baby at home is one of fear. Then the feeling of incredulity creeps up on you – how can anyone let you guys, who are still children, have sole responsibility for this tiny person? Don't worry, these fears are perfectly normal and healthy.

HELP! I'VE HAD A BABY

Being scared is normal. The level of responsibility you now have is probably far greater than any you've previously known. Unless you are a pilot, surgeon or politician at president level it is unlikely that there has been a helpless human dependent upon you for life. Getting the accounts in on time, meeting a deadline or making the right call at work does not compare to this.

- **Stay calm** Your partner may be feeling the stress far more than you. Which is natural, since she's just been through the physical and emotional trauma of giving birth and is now a walking meal tray for this tiny person. Her sleep is interrupted and her emotions all over the place. So you have to calm her down as much as possible.

- **Do everything** around the home. Wash, cook, clean, fetch and carry. Take the baby as much as possible. (Advice on how to handle the bundle is coming up.)

- **Don't party** At least, not yet. Give it a month or so before friends are invited round to meet baby. After all, you and the baby don't really know each other yet, do you?

- **Be there when the midwife visits** Professional post-natal visitors are there to check that all is as it should be in the first few weeks. They'll check the baby but also the mother and you should be there to hear any instructions and advice.

- **Always say when you are going out** and give an approximate length of time for how long you'll be gone. The time that you are away from home can be an

What will a newborn baby look like?

Somebody once remarked that all newborn babies look like Second World War era Winston Churchill (without the cigar, obviously). Which is pretty accurate, regardless of what sex your baby is.

Head Will look too big for its body and slightly pointed for a while. The very top will be soft for 18 months until the skull bones have joined and the hollow between them (fontanelle) disappears.

Eyes May not show their true colour until the age of 6 months. Non-Caucasian babies are usually born with grey/blue eyes. The baby's eyes will be puffy for at least the first three days of its life.

Skin May well look a little patchy for a few days while circulation stabilizes. There may be white spots, due to blocked sebaceous glands, but these will soon clear up. Your baby might look 'hairy' for the first couple of weeks, which is perfectly normal. The hair on its head and shoulders will rub off.

The tag Baby will come home with a plastic peg stuck on its belly button. This will normally fall off, along with the excess bit of the umbilical cord that it is attached to, after a week or two.

anxious one for your partner because she is alone with the baby.

• **Make lists**
a for the shopping – you now have lots of new things to buy that you didn't even know existed before.
b at home – both of you will forget everyday things because you are concentrating so hard on baby. And these simple things, when forgotten, become far more important than they should. Discovering there's no milk for your breakfast at 11.30 p.m. can feel like a major disaster.

DON'T WORRY
All of this anxiety will pass as you both realize that baby is stronger than you think. You might even be that rare breed of new parent who just doesn't get worried by having a tiny, almost alien-looking lifeform sharing your home.

... simple things, when forgotten, become far more important than they should. Discovering there's no milk for your breakfast at 11.30 p.m. can feel like a major disaster.

It's a boy – so deal with it

After the initial rush of adrenalin and joy has drifted away on a sea of serotonin, you are going to start thinking about what exactly it means to have a child, to be the father of ... a boy!?!

I'M A MAN

Being male, you are a man. Full of testosterone, aggression, macho bravado and strong opinions, plus lots of other things. That's true even if you are more like Ned Flanders than Homer Simpson. It's the way men are. When another male presence enters your home and starts making demands of your partner, when she starts showing him more affection and attention than she's giving you, then you feel angry about it. You get resentful towards both this new male presence and your partner, who seems to prefer him to you.

The fact that the male presence is about a foot and a half tall and looks like Winston Churchill makes no difference. He's the one sucking her breasts and getting all those loving strokes on his head while you are told to get dinner, clean the bath and do the shopping (and don't forget the new fella's talcum powder).

Poor, poor you. There you go. You're an adult now.

Six father–baby son dos

1 Do hold him as much as possible. Walk around with him in your arms, and get him to fall asleep on you. You'll soon stop feeling jealous of him that way.

2 Do bath with him lying on your chest. Don't fill the bath too full and keep it warm enough for both of you to be comfortable.

3 Do talk to him as if he's a very special person. Tell him about your favourite team, what happened in your day, everything and anything.

4 Do play him your kind of music. Just don't whack it up to 11 and prepare for him to object to Sonic Youth, 50 Cent or Mantovani – indeed, anything you like, because it's all new to him (except for the stuff you played while he was in the womb).

5 Do take him for drives, properly fastened into his car seat. And don't drive too recklessly.

6 Do wear him in a pouch carrier when playing poker (making sure that no one's smoking). That way he can learn the game early as well as distract the others while you think.

But you know what? You are going to get over this and become a better man, one your son will be proud of when he's old enough to realize what a great guy you are.

IT'S A FATHER–SON THING

This is probably a good time to think for a bit about how you feel about your old man. We went through this back in Chapter 1, but now that you are a dad yourself, it's worth looking at your relationship with your father through fresh eyes. Because it is going to have an effect on your relationship with your son, regardless of how much you might deny it.

In 2001, the US-based website Fathers.com conducted a survey with 1,643 men about their relationship with their father. To the question 'How satisfied were you with your relationship when you were growing up?' fewer than 50% answered that they were 'somewhat satisfied to extremely satisfied' and 53.7% stated they were 'dissatisfied or had mixed feelings'. To the question 'Do you think that most people have unresolved problems with their father?' 55.6% replied that they did.

The most depressing aspect of this survey was that the age group that most strongly agreed with the second question was the 18–24 year-old group (67.2%). Which suggests that, contrary to what we have been led to believe, modern fathering may not have moved on all that much from the previous generation. Perhaps today's fathers aren't as involved in their children's upbringing as we'd like to think.

Fathers.com goes on to point out that 'Income was also a differentiating factor: of respondents making $25,000 or less, 70.1% agreed, compared to only 48.0% among those who make more than $50,000.'

You might find this last statistic quite troubling if you are towards the lower end of the income bracket. But of course this doesn't automatically mean you will have more difficulties in your relationship with your son. While it's true that a family with a lower level of income is going to suffer from more anxieties connected to money issues and long-term security than a more wealthy family, what really matters is how equipped you are to deal with this. Think about your own education. If you were well educated

You get resentful towards both this new male presence and your partner, who seems to prefer him to you.

Six father–baby son don'ts

1 Don't take him to public places in order to pick up women. While his cuteness and your apparent caring attitude will attract women to you in a gallery, park or shopping centre, a story about his mother dying in childbirth will win you lots of sympathy in the beginning only.

2 Don't buy a huge slot car set-up as soon as he's home and expect anyone to believe that you bought it for him.

3 Don't take him to work with you. Your boss might not like it and your son certainly won't. Would you want to go to work at age 3 months?

4 Don't take him to bars, soccer games, gigs or parties where you know there'll be big crowds, people getting drunk and smoking. Wait until he's 14 at least, by which time you'll be trying to stop him from going.

5 Don't dress him in girls' clothes in order to show off your 'enlightened' attitude to gender roles. It will not put him in touch with his feminine side, but it will make people think you are stupid and take pity on him.

6 Don't ever get drunk around him and then try to smother him with kisses or even hold him. Babies can be seriously injured in falls from the smallest heights.

and have a job that which, while not a money-spinner, gives you a good sense of satisfaction, it means you have chosen this path and have opted for creativity and fulfilment over money and (often) a stressful work environment. Chances are you feel happy with this choice and will be able to impart this feeling to your son. There is no reason why the relationship should be strained simply because you don't have a high income.

If you are in the higher income bracket, you are in a privileged position in the sense that you will feel less economic pressure and will feel secure in your ability to be 'head of the family', but you will still need to work hard at your relationship with your son.

More than just a cool fashion accessory, your new child can also help you to win pool games!

It's a girl – so deal with it

After the initial rush of adrenalin and joy has drifted away on a sea of serotonin, you are going to start thinking about what exactly it means to have a child, to be the father of. . . a girl!?!

IT'S A MAN'S, MAN'S WORLD

The feelings that come to a man with the birth of a daughter can be confusing and contradictory. Having never been a girl – forgive the presumption here – a father has no idea of what it feels like to be a daughter. Being a son is ingrained in us, it has formed us. We know how boys think and act, what they want and what they do to get it – which can only add to the fear that we may have about our daughter's life.

Some men (and I realize it's a minority, but sadly they do exist) simply refuse to believe that the child came from their loins since they were so convinced that they could father only male children. These men are not just dumb, but uninformed. The physical process involved in creating a female child is much more complicated than it is for a male. After all, it's easy to put a bunch of spiders, snails and puppy-dog tails together, isn't it?

In their first national poll of fathers, the American website dadsanddaughters.org asked a group of fathers of all ages a range of questions about their relationship with their daughters. The results were not entirely unexpected.

The good news was that 74% of the respondents described their relationship with their daughter as 'excellent with no issues' or 'very good but with a few minor issues'. Interestingly, the fathers who were least likely to say that they enjoyed a good relationship with their daughter had children aged over 26, which suggests that the family unit was no longer living in one place. Physical distance does, naturally, bring pressures of its own.

A cynic could say that of course they'd say they had a good relationship with their daughter, these men read and interact with a website named 'dads and daughters', and so are actively considering it. That cynic would be right, and yes, there are all sorts of other reasons why so many fathers might describe their relationship in this way, not least naivety.

More revealing were the respondents' feelings about the barriers and challenges

Having never been a girl – forgive the presumption here – a father has no idea of what it feels like to be a daughter.

A feeling that you will never have experienced before and that you'll never forget.

Six father–baby daughter dos

1 Do hold her as much as possible. Walk around with her in your arms, and get her to fall asleep on you. You'll be helping to forge a bond with your daughter and allowing your partner some free time.

2 Do bath with her lying on your chest. Don't fill the bath too full and keep it warm enough for both of you to be comfortable.

3 Do talk to her as if she's a very special person. Tell her about your favourite team, what happened in your day, everything and anything.

4 Do play her your kind of music. Just don't whack it up to 11 and be prepared for her to object to Metallica, Ice Cube or Ornette Coleman – or, indeed, anything that you like – because it's all new to her (except for the stuff you played while she was in the womb).

5 Do take her for drives, properly fastened into her car seat. And don't drive too recklessly.

6 Do strap her onto your chest as you walk around, either indoors or out. Smell her head and snuggle with her as you walk, especially in cold weather. (You can and should do this with any baby, not just girls.)

faced by their daughters today. Asked to select from a list of the 'biggest obstacles to a girl's happiness':

- 37% chose unequal treatment or discrimination
- 36% chose popular culture in the form of music, TV and fashion that emphasizes appearance and sex appeal over character and accomplishment (the percentage was largest in the group of fathers of daughters under the age of 12)
- 25% chose the pressure to be thin
- 25% chose physical abuse or harassment

When the fathers were asked what scared them most in regard to their daughters:

- 33% quoted physical or sexual abuse (again, this response was more pronounced among fathers with daughters under 12)
- 22% said the worry that she wouldn't find a man to look after her
- 21% stated the fear that their daughter wouldn't have a loving or equitable relationship with a man

The results show a remarkable unity of hopes and fears among fathers of daughters.

I'd be willing to take a bet on your having been warned about your behaviour towards a man's daughter at least once.

Six father–baby daughter don'ts

1 Don't take her to see movies that are all about cheating guys and the evils that they do to women. Your daughter is too young to be warned against the perils of boyfriends. In fact, she's too young to understand much of what you say.

2 Don't buy a huge slot car set-up as soon as she's home and expect anyone to believe that you bought it to help her break away from pre-ordained gender stereotypes.

3 Don't take her to work with you. Your boss might not like it and she certainly won't. Would you want to go to work at age 3 months?

4 Don't take her to bars, football games, gigs or parties where you know that there are going to be big crowds, people getting drunk and

smoking. Wait until she's 16 at least, by which time you'll have been trying to stop her from going to such places for at least three years.

5 Don't dress her in a mini replica sports team kit in order to show off your 'enlightened' attitude to gender roles. It will not make a life-long fan out of her, but it will make people think you are stupid and take pity on her.

6 Don't ever get drunk around her and then try to smother her with kisses or even hold her. Babies can be seriously injured in falls from the smallest heights.

HOW TO HAVE A HAPPY DAUGHTER

The 2004 poll by dadsanddaughters.org also asked fathers what they thought were the keys to building a better relationship with their daughters. Once again, the answers were positive and reassuring.

More than a third (34%) replied that the key was spending more time with their daughters. This answer was most pronounced among fathers of women aged between 18 and 25, an age at which many women are leaving home, and therefore a time when fathers need to be proactive in order to spend time with them.

Vocalizing a distinctly modern concern (and language), almost a quarter of the men questioned (23%) stated that they thought that if they could 'better communicate [their] thoughts and feelings to her' it would help improve their relationship. Almost as many (22%) responded that they would want to 'do a better job of understanding her point of view'. Which is a distinctly unmasculine thing to do, but certainly an incredibly commendable one.

Perhaps the most surprising but welcome finding from the poll, however, was that almost half (45%) of the men with daughters under the age of 12 agreed that, 'my active involvement [in her life] is vital to her health and well-being'. Daughters flourish in the care of a father who is loving, understanding, non-judgemental and supportive.

Unfortunately it is extremely difficult for all fathers to be all of these things all of the time. But we can try.

Your daughter will always love you, but be kind.

The fathers want to protect their daughters but fear that, once in the world as adults, they will not be able to find the same kind of love and concern from a husband or partner. Which has always been the case. Think back to your relationship with the fathers of past girlfriends and with your father-in-law. I'd be willing to take a bet on your having been warned about your behaviour towards a man's daughter at least once. The worries of fathers are all to do with threats to their daughters' innocence – in the form of music, TV, fashion and peer groups. They might not have felt the same pressures as a boy, but they could all see the effect that pressure to be thin or popular had on girls who were in their peer group.

Don't drop it!

Your partner will have learned some basic baby holds while still in hospital, or from the midwife on home visits. You should certainly have held the baby quite a bit by the time of your paternity leave. But in case you're still a little sketchy on the how-to, here are some pointers.

THE LIFT

When the baby is on its back, slide one hand under the head and neck, with the forearm running down the back. The other hand should slip easily under the baby's lower back. Lift from a position that doesn't harm your back. Make sure that your changing table is at a sufficient height to mean you don't have to bend to change nappies.

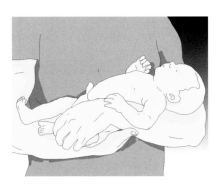

THE CRADLE

The most commonly used hold, here the baby is supported by both hands, with its head upward, in the crook of your arm and close to your breast (don't worry about those sucking faces the baby keeps making even while asleep, it's a reflex and the baby won't

bite you. Not yet, anyway). You can stand and rock slowly or sit easily with the baby in this hold.

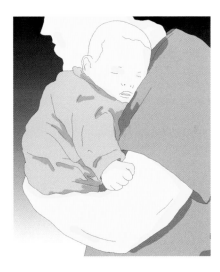

THE SHOULDER HUG

This position can help the baby be winded easily, give it a nice, safe position in which to fall asleep almost upright and allow you to snuggle the head. One hand (it can be either) should support the baby's bottom while the other holds the neck and head. From this position the baby is able to rest its head comfortably on your shoulder and you can ease yourself into a sitting or prone position without waking it.

THE FOOTBALL HOLD

Imagine the baby is a rugby ball and you are holding it in the crook of your arm. The baby's head can be at either end of your arm (in your hand or on your elbow).

If the head is towards your hand, you'll support the baby under the chest and not have your fingers gripped around the neck. If baby's head is towards your elbow, then your hand holds the crotch and the legs can go either side of your arm. It's a good position in which to wash baby's hair – head towards your hand, of course.

FACE OUT

This is not for beginners. Once you've gained confidence in holding the baby – which will probably be after a couple of close drop-calls and many reminders to support the neck – then you'll start 'throwing' the baby around. When the baby's old enough to hold up its own head, the fun will really begin – shoulder rides, upside down and so on. But while the neck muscles are still developing you need to offer full support. In this hold your chest gives the support. One hand holds the baby under its bottom. The baby is facing away from you. Your other hand is holding the baby just under the neck, on the chest. Keep enough pressure on to secure the baby against your chest or abdomen.

INTO THE COT

This might seem difficult, mainly because the aim is to get the baby into the cot without waking, but it isn't. It is essentially a reverse of the Lift (see above). The trick is to keep your body as close to the baby as you lower it – with both hands firmly holding the small of the back and neck and head – gently onto its mattress. Lower yourself with it, slowly drawing your body, that big, warm, safe-feeling place, away from the baby as you gently slide out your hands.

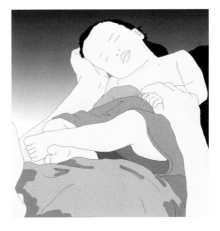

THE LEG CRADLE

Only to be attempted when wide awake. With you lying on your back, your feet flat on the floor, legs together at the knees. Place the baby against your legs, bottom resting on your crotch. You might want a cushion for your head. Always keep one hand on the baby's tummy, or both hands holding the baby under the arms. From this position you can play a rudimentary peek-a-boo with the baby, who'll think that you've lost your head if you lie it flat on the floor while keeping it upright against your legs.

What can go wrong – post-natal depression

Post-natal depression is women's stuff, right? All that hormonal chaos, floods of tears and inability to cope. Men don't have to undergo the rigours of pregnancy and childbirth, so what do they have to moan about? Well, actually, plenty.

REAL MEN GET POST-NATAL DEPRESSION

A staggering number of men get depressed around the birth of a baby. According to research by Dr Simon Lovestone and Professor Kumar at the British Institute of Psychiatry, 25% of men suffer depressive symptoms after the birth of a child. And if a man's partner has PND (which affects one in ten women), then the chance of him also suffering depression rises to almost 50%. Unfortunately, if you're the kind of man a woman would like to have around at the arrival of a new baby – the thoughtful, considerate type who is keen to offer support and sympathy – then you are most likely to suffer from post-natal depression.

> ## 'Social expectations of men often preclude them from feeling able to disclose personal concerns ...'

WHAT'S IT ALL ABOUT?

PND has nothing to do with hormones. It is quantifiably different from the Baby Blues, that short-term hormonal rampage which affects up to 80% of new mothers a few days after giving birth. 'PND is a reactive depression like any other,' says Dr Malcolm George of Queen Mary and Westfield College, London and author of *Postnatal Depression, Relationships and Men.* 'It comes out of life events, particularly negative life events, and can be present when there is a difference between the expectation of things being wonderful and the reality being rather different. Having a baby is not uniformly wonderful.'

Is that shocking news to you? Or, like many men, do you know perfectly well that it's not going to be a bed of roses, but are expert at hiding your own depression and anxiety? 'Social expectations of men often preclude them from feeling able to disclose personal concerns,' says Dr George, adding, 'In order to be valued by others as a "man" they must always be seen to cope.' What's more, as Dr George points out, men are extremely likely to experience rejection – from their partners, from friends, even from some health professionals – if they admit they are depressed. So they bottle it all up and think they'll get over it. Or, worse, think that it's all gone to hell and that they'll have to leave the relationship, the baby and the woman they love.

That's called running away. Which a lot of guys attempt when confronted with a problem that they have no idea how to solve. When men become fathers they are expected

How to spot PND

Answer 'Yes' to more than four and you are probably in the grip of post-natal depression.

1 Are you feeling as if you want your old life back?

2 Do you feel that you can't tell your partner how you feel because it will upset her and make you feel worse?

3 Do you feel jealous of the attention that your partner is showing the baby and not showing you?

4 Are you confused about what you are supposed to be doing and feeling now that you're a father?

5 Do you keep making excuses about having to work longer and put off going home?

6 Are you drinking too much?

A staggering number of men get depressed around the birth of a baby.

- Pay attention when a professional offers you advice about PND. Whether it's the head of a parenting class, a midwife or a home visitor (they are qualified and see this a lot) or even a friend who has been there and done that, take advice on board and consider it carefully. Do not dismiss any ideas out of hand – your depression might be making you bloody-minded.

- Talk to your partner about how you feel, but do not blame her (or the baby). Blaming will only cause recriminations and blow up into huge arguments that will add to your depression. Ask her to listen to what you have to say, tell her that you know that it isn't her fault and are not blaming her. Just that you think that you need help. The mere act of discussing how you feel can help alleviate some of the depression.

- Talk to your best friend or close family about how you feel. Sharing a load can lighten it, and their support can really help you.

- Exercise. Get those endorphins flowing. You can pound away resentment and anger as you run or pump.

to do many things: provide for the family financially, offer their partners unstinting practical and emotional support, love the baby and share fully in its care. Of course we all want to do this, but it's hard, right?

WHAT TO DO ABOUT IT

- If you are feeling unable to cope and think you might be really depressed, see your doctor. It might be that you need a short-term course of antidepressants.

- Don't despair. This will pass. It may be hard to imagine right now, and what do I know, I'm just a book, but it will pass.

POST-NATAL DEPRESSION IN WOMEN

Depression among new mothers is unfortunately very common. Thankfully, most sufferers tend to recover in a matter of weeks, but it can last months, or even years. You can help with the recovery from PND by first identifying the symptoms and then actively doing something about it. It is important that you don't confuse the more common Baby Blues – that affects up to 80% of all new mothers – with PND. The Baby Blues are connected to hormonal changes brought about by the birth rather than any psychological problem. They will most commonly result in your partner feeling 'low' for a week to 10 days after the birth and be accompanied by a few tearful episodes. A feeling of being unable to cope is common among sufferers of the BBs, as are mood swings, irritability and indecision. However, these occurrences are usually fleeting and minor in comparison with PND.

Surprise her with flowers and gifts (try not to look too guilty, though).

THE SIGNS OF PND IN WOMEN

Some of the symptoms of PND are common among new mothers who aren't actually suffering from it, but if a number of these symptoms are present then there is a good chance that your partner has post-natal depression.

- Bursting into tears without any apparent reason.

- Feelings of hopelessness and despondency. These can be expressed in terms of not wanting to do anything other than sit at home, refusing offers of assistance and negative responses to everything.

If she has trouble discussing her condition with you, get a friend or relative to talk to her. It's important that she ... doesn't feel isolated.

- Panic attacks for no clear reason (yes, I know this can happen a lot).

- Sleeplessness, even when the baby is sleeping well.

- Loss of sexual libido.

- Obsessive behaviour such as cleaning persistently, replacing objects in the same spot, repeated washing of hands.

- Lack of concentration – inability to read, watch a whole movie or finish a conversation.

- Permanent expressions of guilt over any little thing, from spilling milk to 'being a bad mother'.

- Lack of self-esteem.

WHAT YOU CAN DO TO HELP

- Persuade your partner to talk to her doctor about her depression. She may be given antidepressants for a short period.

- Make sure that the doctor also gives your partner a physical examination and assures her that aches and pains are a normal part of recovery from giving birth.

- Let her rest as much as possible. Take the baby and let her sleep during the day if she is having trouble sleeping at night.

- Make sure that you are all eating properly. Fresh fruit and vegetables are a great aid to mental and physical health. Junk food is a depressant.

- Do not drink alcohol with her or in front of her. Despite bringing an initial feeling of euphoria, alcohol kills important vitamins and hangovers make everyone depressed.

- Help her to exercise gently. Take walks with the baby, preferably in pleasant surroundings. If you live in an inner-city area, drive to somewhere that has green scenery and walk there.

- Surprise her with gifts and flowers and expressions of love and devotion.

- Talk to her about her depression and reassure her that it will pass.

- If she has trouble discussing her condition with you, get a friend or relative to talk to her. It's important that she shares her emotional troubles with other people and doesn't feel isolated.

Baby bonding

One of the most likely ways you can beat your PND is to bond with your baby. By forming a close emotional tie in the first few weeks of the baby's life, a father can get a lot of fulfilment and a sense of well-being out of the experience of being a dad. The baby will enjoy it, too. As will your partner, because your bonding will give her a physical break from caring for the child, as well as immense satisfaction that father and baby are getting on well.

Be physical. Hold the baby as much as possible in the first few weeks of its life. Skin to skin contact is incredibly rewarding for both of you.

Carry baby. Whenever possible, if going out with baby in a harness, try to wear it on your chest rather than your back. The closeness of the baby's head to your nose can only induce warm, protective feelings towards your child.

Be inclusive. Don't ignore the baby when you're doing the simplest of things, such as watching TV or listening to music. While the baby won't be able to make out the plot of *The Sopranos*, the sound and light issuing from the set will offer some amusement. Likewise with music, you can dance and sing with baby.

Feed baby. As soon as possible, which won't be for a few weeks unless your partner is having trouble with breast-feeding, you should be giving the baby its milk via a (sterilized) bottle. It doesn't matter whether the milk is expressed mother's milk or formula, the experience of holding the baby while it feeds is unique.

Talk to baby. Just as you did when the baby was in your partner's womb, you should be talking to the baby, making cooing noises, singing to it and looking at its face as you make (nice) noises.

Sleep

We've touched on the possible problems of sleep in earlier chapters, but now that you have a baby at home you are beginning to discover what the phrase 'sleep deprivation' really means. Or maybe you are lucky and your child sleeps for seven or eight hours straight through pretty much from the age of two weeks. In which case, you are a rare breed (though it does not mean that your next child will follow the same sleep pattern).

MOTHER AND CHILD SLEEP UNION

Your baby has no conception of time, so doesn't know the difference between night and day. Think back to when you were in your early 20s and living with pals. Take out the sex, drugs and rock 'n' roll and that's what the baby is feeling. It only knows when it is hot, cold, wet or hungry. Oh, and whether its mother and source of food and sustenance is near or not. So baby sleeps in the same room and more than likely the same bed as its mother. Which is the one that you used to share, remember?

THE BED SET-UP

Many couples opt for the sleeping arrangement whereby baby is in a Moses basket on a stand close to the mother's side of the bed. Close enough so that when baby

wakes at 3 a.m. and wants to feed, mother can simply reach over, take baby out of the basket and lay it next to her to feed. When baby's fed and asleep again, mother can lift it back into the Moses basket. All without disturbing your beauty sleep. Hey, it might happen once or twice.

What's more likely, though, is that baby will mewl in the basket, waking both of you from the shallow sleep that you've become used to never getting beyond by Night 3. Mother will lift baby into your bed, possibly into the middle, and attempt to feed. Baby will feed for just long enough to allow you to drift off. Then baby will cry. Loudly. You will have to get up, take baby in your arms and walk around, burping baby until all goes quiet again.

When baby is asleep in your arms, possibly after 20 minutes of your pacing about and gently rocking on your heels (lift an arm and let it fall – any resistance means

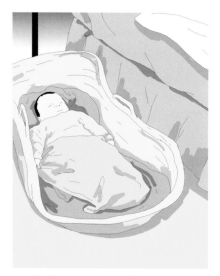

How the Moses basket works in your room.

that baby's still awake), you can put baby down in the Moses basket. Now you can get back into bed for another hour or two of shallow sleep. Before it all happens again.

YOUR PARTNER'S SLEEP

The baby's mother will undoubtedly benefit from getting snatches of sleep whenever possible. You are the best person to make that happen. Remember that she has had a physical as well as emotional shock in giving birth. She may need to heal physically, a process aided by sleep and relaxation, both of which are precious commodities when a small baby is in your home. To help her get this rest, take the baby for walks, shopping or to a game on weekend afternoons, and also when you get home from work, which also helps your bonding process. When baby needs burping during the night, get up and walk around with her while your partner drifts back to sleep.

YOUR SLEEP

There is no doubt that a lack of sleep can adversely affect your ability to function at work. Research shows that by losing sleep you lose intelligence (at least, your IQ drops) and have trouble communicating because your brain and mouth are not in the same gear and become forgetful. Which is not impressive, is it?

Hopefully your boss and workmates are going to be a little understanding about your condition. However, if your sleep-deprived idiocy persists beyond the first month, you may find that sympathy and understanding start to wane.

WHAT TO DO

There are a number of adjustments you can

Is baby going to sleep in your bed?

4

THE CASE FOR

| Your partner won't have to get up in order to lift baby into bed to feed.

| You will have the pleasure of waking up with your beautiful new baby, further cementing the growing bond between you.

THE CASE AGAINST

| If baby sleeps in your bed, your sleep will be more disturbed than if it is in a Moses basket, because it is going to kick, whimper and rustle during

sleep. This will keep you awake and may lead to your waking the baby to check that everything is OK. Thus disrupting everyone's sleep.

| You run the risk of rolling onto the baby. Especially if you drink heavily or are on medication that puts you into a deep sleep.

| Baby will get used to your bed and not want to go into its own.

| Sex will prove impossible for even longer. Or at least sex in your bed, at night, will.

---

make to home and work life that will help you get as much quality sleep as possible at night during baby's early weeks, and catch those invaluable snooze moments during the day.

MOVE INTO THE SPARE ROOM
This is the time you will really appreciate that you live in a place with a spare bedroom. As long as your partner agrees, you can move into the spare room during the working week and get some decent shut-eye. It's going to be tough on her, having to cope with the baby at night, but you are going to make up for that by:

- Being the parent who rises during the night at weekends.

- Coming home from work on time during the week and taking over the care and attention of the baby for at least an hour.

- Meeting your partner and baby for lunch during the week at least twice and taking care of the baby while the mother eats, shops or does whatever the hell she wants.

- Buying flowers and presents irregularly, but often, for mother and baby.

SLEEP ON THE JOB
Taking naps can help you as much as your partner. If you are sticking with the same bed (even with baby, too) and enduring broken sleep, you should take sleep when and as it becomes possible.

Research shows that by losing sleep you lose intelligence (at least, your IQ drops) and have trouble communicating because your brain and mouth are not in the same gear and you become forgetful. Which is not impressive, is it?

- Lunchtime nap. If you drive to work and have a quiet car park (preferably in the shade), you can take a sleep in your car at lunchtime. And if you work close to home, you can always pop back to your empty bed for a snooze when possible.

- Round and around. If you live in a city with an underground rail network that has a 'circle' line, get on the train and go around a few times, catching a nap as you go. Do not take your wallet, watch or anything that could tempt muggers.

- Nature's tonic. If you work near countryside or a river, during the summer months you could walk to a shady spot under a tree and snooze.

WORK THROUGH IT

Actually, let's face it, you're not going to do any of the above, are you? Being a man, you'll try to tough it out, keep awake and work through it all. So here are some tips to help you make the best of it. (If your job involves driving, use of firearms or operating big machines, do not attempt to tough out a lack of sleep. What are you, nuts? Someone could get seriously hurt by your stupid attitude. You need your sleep!)

- Make sure that your workstation is near a window or air-conditioning unit. Keep the window open in all weather and the AC turned to chilly. Or buy a desk fan.

- Always carry a notebook and write down everything that you're asked to do. Tick each task as you complete it.

- Drink lots of water (1.5 to 2 litres a day). Sports drinks are also good. Frequent trips to the toilet will keep you awake.

- Don't eat heavy lunches – stay hungry.

- Exercise at lunchtimes if you're not going to sleep.

- If your work has a shower, take one after lunch, when you'll be at your most sleepy.

- Get up and walk around, taking screen breaks (if you work with a computer) or breaks from your workstation. You are entitled to them by law in any case.

- Keep your desk or workstation full of stuff that would be very uncomfortable if you put your head down on it. Spikes and heavy-duty staplers are a good idea ...

Sex ... or not?

While we're in bed, or not, as the case might be, the thorny subject of postnatal sex might as well be dealt with. In an ideal world both you and your partner would resume your sex life as if you hadn't witnessed a baby enter the world through her vagina. But when was this world ever ideal?

WHEN WILL IT BE POSSIBLE?

The short answer is, when she's ready. Naturally a woman will go off sex after giving birth. She may well have gone off you, too, for a while. How long she is 'off' sex can vary, though, from a matter of a couple of weeks (if you're lucky) to a couple of years (it has been known). And there's no point pestering her for sex, either. It'll just make matters worse. Do you want a relationship where she has all the sexual power, the right to grant you sexual favours when and as she pleases?

MENTALLY POSSIBLE

You might have to clear your mind of a few images from the birth before you're ready for sex with your partner. Which is just as well, because that means you're not going to be bothering her for sex as soon as she gets back from the hospital. Likewise, she has to get her mind round the thought of engaging in the act again, too. If either of you is suffering from post-natal depression (see pages 134–138), you're not going to feel like it, either. If it's just her suffering PND, then you know not to ask.

PHYSICALLY POSSIBLE

It depends on what kind of birth your partner had. If it involved stitches then you are not going to be having penetrative sex for a month or more at least after the removal of the stitches. So be inventive with your sexual play (see below).

> **Naturally a woman will go off sex after giving birth. She may well have gone off you, too, for a while.**

Another way

Think differently

What is it with you that it all has to be penetrative, anyway? If you think a little differently and take things easy, you just might find that there are a number of sexually satisfying activities other than intercourse. And that doesn't just mean blow jobs, either. Extended foreplay, mutual masturbation, oral sex can all be just as pleasurable.

Try a little tenderness

Be romantic. Make like it's your first time (and hers). Discuss what she wants you to do – you can make it dirty – and only do that. Keep telling her that she's sexy – one of the most common reasons for women not wanting to have sex after childbirth is that they don't think you find them sexually attractive.

Be prepared

First, for it to be a little less than earth-moving for both of you. Second, if you are going to have intercourse, use birth control. Just because she's had one baby doesn't mean she won't very easily conceive another. You may also find that you need more lubricant than before childbirth.

Improvise

If you are both up for having sex and the baby's asleep in your bed, you are not going to risk waking baby by moving it into the Moses basket, are you? So try making love somewhere else – the kitchen, the stairs, the living-room couch, the dining table, wherever. You could be adventurous and arrange a night out, get a babysitter for an hour or two and book a motel or hotel room. You can even book in as Mr and Mrs, truthfully for once.

Pray to Onan

You know by now that it doesn't make you blind. After all, self-love is better than no love at all. If you need outside stimuli to get you going, make sure that your partner is aware of what you're doing and doesn't object. Many a relationship has foundered on a fast Internet connection to porn sites.

Hello Grandpa

In some ways, it's going to be easier to talk to your father now than it was before the birth. It might even be easier to talk to your father-in-law, too. Not that it's a foregone conclusion.

These days men such as you can be much more connected and involved with their children than your father's generation was – remember? The new grandpas (assuming that there are two) may well react very differently to your new state of fatherhood, and there are no guarantees this will be in the way you want them to. Here are three main things for you to consider about the grandpas at this stage, and they all require you to think before reacting.

LOOK

Watch the expression on the new grandpa's face as he is offered his new grandchild to hold. If he looks delighted then great, you have someone and something new to talk about with him. He loves the new member of the family.

If he looks apprehensive, don't force him into holding the baby. Let him approach the matter in his own time. Talk to him as you hold the baby and take note of where he's looking – if it's at the baby and not you, don't feel offended, that's good. He's familiarizing himself with the baby.

If he looks appalled at the idea of holding a newborn baby (or any baby under a year old) then don't push the matter. If grandpa was an uninvolved father and he wants to be a similarly uninvolved grandpa – he might even hate the idea of grandpahood – then there's nothing that you can do at this stage. You've got other stuff to deal with. Or of course it could be that he just feels awkward, and this may well be overcome with time and encouragement.

LISTEN

If grandpa wants to coochy-coo at baby, or you, then let him. If grandpa wants to recall your or your partner's babyhood, then let him. He's almost as emotionally overcome at the birth of your child as you were and this is a prime bonding moment for all three of you (or four, or five, etc.).

If grandpa is finding it hard to talk about the baby, help him. It's OK for you to babble about your new status as a dad, but you should listen to what he has to say and try to talk to him about his thoughts on the matter. He might profess a feeling of guilt that he wasn't more involved when his children were small, which is quite common, and to which the usual reply (a good one) is that times were different then.

If grandpa prefers to ignore the baby altogether, then talk to him about whatever he's willing to bring up. Try not to resent the fact that your dad/partner's dad isn't besotted by this bundle of joy in your arms. It is important that you don't alienate him, which may happen if you force him into confronting the baby in a way that is uncomfortable for him.

LEARN

Any grandpa who's immediately involved with a baby grandchild probably has some parenting advice that is worth listening to. Even a grandpa who's not sure about how to handle a baby can have something worthwhile to contribute to your knowledge of what is, after all, new to you.

A grandpa who seems to resent or even be afraid of the situation still has wisdom to impart. Learn from his mistakes and don't repeat them. Feel his fear, see if you recognize it and, if you do, confront it and conquer it.

Any grandpa who's immediately involved with a baby grandchild probably has some parenting advice that is worth listening to.

Hello Grandma

Traditionally, mothers have had more involvement in the raising of children than their partners. Mothers have also traditionally had more to say about their children's adult relationships, their children's marriages and ultimately their grandchildren. By now you should have a pretty good idea of what your partner's relationship with her mother is like. You'll also know where you stand with your mother-in-law. Or at least you thought you did. Obviously, all of the advice given about grandpas on the previous couple of pages

goes for grandmas, too, but the relationship between grandma and your new family is going to be different.

AVOID THE MOTHER-IN-LAW WAR

Both grandmas will expect the same kind of access to their grandchild and you have to do as much as possible to make sure that this happens. In the first few months of the baby's life your partner may feel that she needs maternal support and so may want to have her own mother around more than

Try to avoid scenes like this between grandmothers. You might find it funny, but no one else will.

yours. If this is the case then you have to discuss the matter with your mother and you must either make sure that she understands the situation and is happy with it, or else accept that you have to lie to her. A little white lie in this case is wholly appropriate. Your family life is already fraught enough without having to worry about a grandma being upset at spending a day or two less with the baby than her counterpart. So don't tell her. Or at least underplay the amount of time that your mother-in-law is spending with baby. Make sure that your partner approves of the lie before telling it, of course.

Be prepared for grandmas to offer contrasting advice about bringing up baby. As long as you and your partner have your own plan for raising children (as much as anyone has) and are agreed on the main points, such as sleep training (see page 161) eating (see page 160) and discipline (see page 174), then you can take or leave grandma's advice as you wish. In order to minimize any possible friction between grandmas, it's best not to pass any parenting advice between them – especially if it's contrasting advice. Answering one grandma's query about why you're doing something in a particular way with, 'Because that's how [the other grandma] says to do it,' is not a good idea.

VISITING RIGHTS

If you or your partner has a tricky relationship with one (or more) of the grandparents, then you will need to decide between you the level of involvement you want that grandparent to have with baby. If it is to be none at all then you have to be prepared to stick to the decision no matter what and prepare for ostracism from that side of the family. Also

Grandma in the attic

Something best avoided if possible – and it should always be possible – is to have one of the grandmas move into your home just after the birth. Or before, come to that. Unless you entered into the relationship with your partner in the full knowledge that you would also be living with her mother, or yours, then it should not happen. If, in the event of a traumatic birth, say, a grandma is needed to stay with you until your partner is well enough to cope alone, then the period that she is with you should be set and adhered to.

be prepared to explain to your child why there is only one grandma (or only one grandpa) when other people have more. This explanation will probably be needed sooner than you'd expected or hoped.

Hopefully, however, both sets of grandparents will be happy to see their grandchild at a time and place that suits everyone involved. You will probably find yourself visiting alternate grandparents during holiday times.

5 Getting in gear

AFTER THE FIRST COUPLE OF MONTHS YOUR LIFE WILL SEEM TO HAVE
REACHED A PLATEAU OF NORMALITY. SO IT'S TIME TO DO THINGS WITH
YOUR BABY THAT YOU LIKE DOING. BETTER STILL, IT'S TIME TO HIRE
SOME CHILDCARE AND DO THINGS THAT YOU ENJOY WITHOUT BABY!

Childcare

When it comes to choosing outside help to care for your children, it is preferable to use family. However, in contrast to previous generations, this is no longer the norm. And it's a shame. Having to employ strangers to care for a 3-month-old baby is often necessary and certainly not wrong, especially when that stranger is properly trained and has great references. It's just that the stranger is highly unlikely to be around for very long, whereas a grandparent or aunt is going to be a part of the child's future.

WHY CHILDCARE?

With maternity and paternity leave being so meagre in so many Western countries, there is every chance that a mother will have to return to work within 3 to 6 months of giving

---

The hand that rocks the cradle

If you have to hire a nanny for your child, then make sure that she (although there are increasing numbers of men taking up the profession) has the correct training certificates and follow up all references in person. At interviews make sure that she is in tune with your ideas of parenting and isn't just agreeing in order to get a job – usually one can tell; watch out for evasive eye contact and head turned to the left when answering 'uncomfortable' questions. Don't even let her past the door if she smokes (you can smell it). Although an interest in her wages is to be expected, too much enthusiasm about what she's to be paid and when can suggest that money is of more importance to her than the baby.

If you are contemplating having a live-in nanny, think carefully. You already have one stranger in your home (the baby, dummy), do you really want another? Especially a young woman who may trek to the bathroom in scanty clothing at a time when you may not have had sex for some time? I'm not suggesting that any live-in nanny would want to have sex with you; rather, I'm trying to save you the embarrassment of a failed seduction. Do you want the guilt of fantasizing about another woman who shares your bathroom while your partner is still suffering from giving birth to your child?

At interviews make sure that she is in tune with your ideas of parenting and isn't just agreeing in order to get a job ...

birth. Increasingly, mothers and even fathers are choosing to alter their working patterns in order to care for and be with their children. However, there are still a huge number of parents who both need to work, either to feed the family or for professional reasons. These people have to hire childcare while they work. There are four distinct types of childcare available.

NURSERY CARE

There are a number of professional and state-run day nurseries that cater for children from the age of 3 months. There are also a number of unprofessional day-care nurseries operating. While a nursery place is usually cheaper than hiring a sole-charge nanny, the effects on the baby are unfortunately more detrimental. Since at the nursery there will be three or more children to every adult, your child is not going to have constant adult supervision. Research has shown that children who are put into day-care from an early age become institutionalized and suffer more insecurity than children who enjoy one-on-one care. While children who attend nurseries from infancy can appear to be more social and 'mature', it seems that what has in fact happened is that they have adapted their behaviour to attract adult attention, of which they are relatively starved.

The nursery will probably have a high level of occupational, learning and play equipment on hand. This is great for a child who can crawl or walk, but before the age of 6 months your baby is not going to be able to do either.

CHILDMINDER

There may be someone living in your neighbourhood who looks after pre-school children in her home for a fee. This person will be kind and attentive, but she will also probably have many other children to care for and is unlikely to have much child-centred learn-and-play equipment. She will undoubtedly be cheaper than a nursery or nanny, though.

NANNY CARE

Employing an individual to look after your baby is expensive and there are different concerns from those relating to nursery care. However, if you get the right nanny the results can be beneficial to you and baby both. You get peace of mind – and perhaps even a new friend – while your baby gets 100% attention and care from one person.

FAMILY CARE

Having a grandma or aunt (or even cousin or best friend) to care for your child is undoubtedly the best possible childcare option. As well as the minimal cost (presumably), there is the invaluable fact of knowing that your baby is being cared for by someone who loves it, someone who is hopefully going to be in its life for many years to come.

If your relationship with one or both of the grandmas is such that you are able to have them either singly, together or alternately take care of your baby while you both work, then this is ideal. If you live in the same area as one of the grandmas and she has the time and inclination to care for the baby, then great. However, you must maintain constant dialogue with her about how you are raising your child. She must agree with what she might think are new-fangled ways of parenting, and she must carry out your wishes. This is possibly where the relationship might falter, of course. When you are employing a trained stranger as a nanny, then you can give orders that have to be obeyed. When it's your mother or mother-in-law, you probably can't issue orders and she may well believe that Nanny knows best.

It's a tough call and only you and your partner can make it.

Making a choice about your baby's childcare is not easy. You are unlikely to get it right first time. Or even second time. The best thing to do is whatever you think is best, even if that might seem the hardest thing to do. If you can't live on the wages of just you or your partner, then look at changing your life so that you can. Get a new job, move house to be near family who can care for baby, and do whatever you can in order to ensure that you can both be with your child as much as possible.

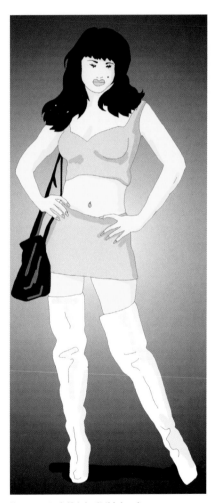

Nanny material? I don't think so!

Quality time

If both you and your partner are working all day and only get to see your baby at night and at weekends, then pretty much any time that you both spend with baby is going to be quality time. However, it can be hard for a guy to realize that the time you are with your non-speaking, walking or crawling child is of high quality. But it is. Here's how:

PLAYING ON THE CARPET

Baby will probably have a hanging toy contraption, an arrangement of straps, bells and mirrors that hang from a small, padded bar which is placed directly over baby on her sheepskin rug. If you have neither, get them now. Babies love lying on (real) sheepskins rugs, and they love playing with things that hang above them from the age of 3 months. You will get an incredible amount of enjoyment out of playing with this contraption and your baby on the carpet.

WALKING

Hopefully you have a harness-style carrying contraption in which you can strap baby to your chest. With this on, you can walk about and talk to baby. No one will think that you're mad. You get exercise and you both get fresh air. When you take the carrier off after an hour or more, you will feel physically bereft.

WATCHING TV

Of course your baby doesn't get all the intricacies of a ball game, or the nuances of some *Seinfeld* gags, but she does 'get' your excitement and laughter. She also registers the changing colours on the TV. Sit her on

your lap, either upright, head against your chest, or lying across a cushion on your lap, and tickle as required.

AT THE GAME

It's a good idea to get baby used to the ritual of going to a game with dad as soon as possible. Having a baby strapped to your chest should ensure that you are given some space when getting to your seat and if you go just with baby, you might well find that some accommodating soul around you is willing to fetch food and hot drinks. Again, your excitement and enjoyment will transfer to baby and it doesn't matter how much noise baby makes. Remember to take food for baby with you.

EXERCISE

If you jog then get one of those jogging buggies for baby (if you can afford it). You'll find baby either giggling madly as you rush around, or falling fast asleep with the motion. It's great for the efficiency of your exercise, too, what with all that extra weight to carry.

ART GALLERIES

At last, someone who'll listen to your amateur art criticism without objection!

READING

Remember that baby likes the sound of your voice. You can read anything, from Dostoevsky to Elmore Leonard, it doesn't matter. Baby will love the even reading tone and modulation of your voice and you get to read a book. When did that last happen?

SNOOZE

Once you have had a snooze on the sofa with baby asleep on your chest you will not have to ask what quality time is. In fact, when baby gets too old to fall asleep on you, you'll physically miss it. The sense of trust engendered by such a small and helpless creature falling asleep on you is almost overwhelming.

And baby came too

Once you get beyond the first 3 months of baby's life you may well wonder why anyone told you that your social life would change once you had children. There is little reason why new parents should not have a perfectly busy social life. OK, so it's not always that easy, but you don't have to give up your former activities altogether.

THE PORTABLE GUEST

With a good child car seat ensemble, you'll find that you can take baby pretty much anywhere with you. Since for the first few months baby only wants to eat and sleep, as long as there's the means to do both, baby really won't care where she is. A car seat that can be lifted straight out of the motor without removing baby is a must-have, though.

THE PERFECT DINNER GUEST

You will probably have friends who are childless and may be unfamiliar with how a child of 3-12 months behaves. These same friends will probably live in adult-oriented homes, and worry what a baby could do to their belongings. Once you've made them aware that a baby of that age doesn't actually 'do' anything, they will invite you to dinner. Of course you can go, even if the dinner party is unlikely to finish before 3 a.m. and the dessert won't reach the table until around midnight. That's if you are up to it. Baby won't care as long as mum's around when food is required. In fact, baby will love the dinner. Baby is the perfect dinner guest because she will offer amusement and conversation without eating anything or getting drunk.

After getting admiring looks and praise from all around the table for an hour or so, baby can retire to the baby seat or, if you've brought it, the Moses basket for a few hours' sleep. On leaving, if baby's still asleep, there's no need to wake her.

EATING OUT WITH BABY

As a general rule, smart restaurants don't cater for babies, so ask when attempting to book a table. Some restaurants positively encourage parents to bring children, but that is usually for lunch. They may have a different policy in the evenings.

You shouldn't take baby to fast-food restaurants at all. Ever. That's because you shouldn't be eating there yourself. Ever.

You are probably not going to want to eat at a bar or pub because of the cigarette smoke that usually hangs over each table, even in the 'no-smoking' zone.

Baby is the perfect dinner guest because she will offer amusement and conversation without eating anything or getting drunk.

BABY EATING WHILE YOU'RE OUT

If your partner is breast-feeding baby and you are at lunch in a public place, then remember that she is legally allowed to breast-feed anywhere. However, if you are with friends who may be embarrassed by the act, it's your duty to distract them with witty conversation while baby chows down.

HOLIDAYING WITH BABY

A small (pre-toddler-age) baby is so portable that you can holiday pretty much anywhere you like. If you're staying local, then your car will carry everything that you need – you'll soon learn to pack less in order to get everything for baby in.

- If you're flying anywhere then remember that a child under the age of 2 is entitled to free flights and will be strapped onto a parent's lap for the duration. You can usually carry baby on board in the car seat, which can of course be used in the rental car at your holiday destination. Pushchairs and strollers will have to be put into the hold, though.

- If staying in a hotel, make sure that the staff know what age your baby is when you book. It would be terrible to be turned away at the reception desk because they don't cater for babies. If staying at a villa or house, make sure that the owners know that you have a baby with you and ask for all baby-related fixtures to be available (high chair, crib, etc.).

- If holidaying in a hot country, take a lot of heavy-duty sun screen, hats and all-in-one bathing suits for baby. Only use bottled water.

- Do not take baby white-water rafting, paragliding, extreme ironing or surfing.

Baby's first year

For the first 3 months of your baby's life you probably didn't notice too much change in her. When changing nappies you will have noticed that her poo became a different colour and consistency (and smell), and she will have grown bigger of course. She might have lost some hair and then gained some more, but she didn't move too much of her own free will. That will change throughout her first year.

AGED UP TO 3 MONTHS

- For the first 8 weeks of her life baby's hands were almost permanently curled into a tiny fist. Now they have opened up.

- She can see things at about a foot away, shake a rattle and watch her hands as she plays.

- By the end of the third month baby has realized that she can make things happen by hitting or interacting in some way with them – like those hanging bells and things on her floor bar toy.

- Baby has begun to make noises such as gurgles, etc. This is because you and your partner have been constantly talking to her.

- By 3 months baby can 'hold' her head as she is lifted, rather than letting it flop alarmingly backwards. She has completely uncurled and can kick (and enjoys it, too).

- By the end of the third month she can roll from her back onto her side or from her front onto her side and then onto her back. Which is why she should never be left on a high surface.

Baby should be introduced to a bottle by the end of the third month as well as being fed from the breast (hopefully mother can express milk for the bottle).

AGED UP TO 6 MONTHS

- By the fourth month baby can focus on objects that are far away and is able to follow them with her eyes if they move, moving her head as the object travels. She knows where her hand is, and can grab things straight away. Unfortunately, everything usually goes into her mouth.

- Baby will babble and say 'Aaah' and maybe 'Maaa' ('Daaa' is more difficult).

- By 6 months baby should begin to be weaned from the breast or bottle. Her diet can begin to change, with cow's milk being added to bottles. A cup, with juice or water, can be introduced at between 4 and 5 months. Solid foods can be introduced at 6 months and there should be a move towards baby having only three proper feeds a day, at roughly the same time as the adults. It's a good idea to cut out the middle of the night feed by 6 months.

- By 6 months baby can sit up unaided, is trying to pull herself up, can get her feet under her body and lift herself up with them. This is the beginning of baby mastering the crawl.

AGED UP TO 9 MONTHS
- Baby's first tooth should pop out at 7 months, with four top teeth appearing at 8 months.

- Baby will be sitting upright unaided, using hands for balance, by 8 months, and crawling around at 9 months.

- Despite not being able to talk, baby will follow a sound, such as her name being spoken, to the source of the sound.

- Baby has added an extra syllable to her 'words' by 8 months, so is saying 'Maala' and 'Aahga' and so on. Interestingly, baby will follow an adult conversation that is not directed at her, with her head moving towards each speaker in turn.

AGED UP TO 12 MONTHS
- By the end of her first year, baby can 'stand' on her own legs, with her feet flat, knees straight and supporting herself by holding on to something, such as a chair

or table leg. She will have found her balance at 10 to 11 months.

- By 11 months she'll be able to pull herself up but not sit down. Which may lead to some strange crying fits – so if your baby's been standing for a while and is seemingly happy but then bursts into tears, it's because she's just realized that she's stuck. Help her down. Then she'll pull herself up again ...

- At 10 to 11 months baby will begin to use sounds to mean objects, and to imitate words as sounds fairly accurately. She might not have spoken too many words, but she will probably know them by now. It just takes a little longer for her to get them out. She'll be calling you 'dad' pretty soon.

- By 12 months baby will be able to cruise around the room, walking sideways and holding on to things such as chairs, tables, your legs, as she identifies her support.

Feed me

You should have been giving baby a bottle by the third month of her life, and a cup by the fifth month. If your partner has been back at work from the sixth month then baby should definitely be also eating solid foods by that point.

BABY'S FIRST FOODS

The first 'solid' foods that baby will take to are not that solid, really. Mashed-up bananas, cereal and fruit or vegetable purées don't call for the use of teeth, which is why they're good. Rusks, bread crusts and biscuits will help baby with teething as well as give her nourishment, so they can be added to baby's diet from 6 months. Make sure that whatever you give your baby is as pure and free from additives as possible. There is a wide range of organic baby foods in jars available at most supermarkets. Choose them when possible, and go for as many flavours as you can. It's a good idea to introduce your baby to as wide a range of tastes as soon as possible. Do not give baby chips to suck on – they're full of fat and usually salt, which is bad for her. Why are you eating that crap, anyway?

GETTING MESSY

Be prepared to get dirty when baby is feeding. A baby can suck from birth, it's a reflex action, but chewing and swallowing are things that she'll learn. So lots will come out of her mouth just after it's gone in, and that's natural. Table manners will come much later; for the first year of eating solids just aim to get as much of it into baby's stomach as goes on the floor, in your face or in baby's hair. If you don't enjoy cleaning the floor after every meal, put newspaper under and around baby's chair while she's eating.

BE REGULAR

Although a baby will need to eat more often than you, you should still feed baby when you eat. It's a very good habit to get into (families should always eat together when possible) and teaches her a regular eating pattern. Just make sure that she gets carrots and apples and so on between meals.

BE HEALTHY

All of you should eat five portions of fresh fruit and vegetables a day. Just remember that her portions are much smaller than yours. Don't eat fast food. Don't eat TV dinners. Cook yourself whenever possible (and it's always possible).

Sleep easy

5

The patterns and benefits of sleep for you and your partner were covered in Chapter 3. This section is to help you get baby into a good sleep pattern. However, you may have to read several books about sleep training before you hit the right one for your baby.

NIGHT FEEDS

Some night feeds end after only a few months because baby is sleeping through. Other parents find that the night feed is the best for baby because everyone is rested and there are no distractions (and the night feed can go on for a year or more). If your baby enjoys the night feed too much, you are likely to have more trouble getting her to sleep through. So attempt to stop the night feed as soon as possible after baby is on solid food, tough as it might be. Getting baby to eat well before bed should help.

TIME FOR BED

It's a good idea to develop a bedtime routine as early as possible. A typical routine will involve bath, pyjamas, a story, putting baby in her crib and a lullaby. Some parents find such a routine so enjoyable that they attempt to carry it on well into their child's teen years. This is not recommended.

DON'T BE NAP HAPPY

Although small children will need to take an afternoon nap until well into their toddler years, it's a good idea for such naps to be taken at a regular hour. Don't let your children fall asleep too close to bedtime, as you'll simply have to wake them to get them to bed, which is silly and disruptive.

GET ANOTHER ROOM

If getting your baby to sleep has been problematic and requires you or your partner being with her as she drifts off, then getting baby into her own room to sleep is going to be hard. But you need to try. Baby should ideally sleep in her own cot from the earliest age (even in your room). A baby that sleeps with its parents is going to have greater separation problems than one that doesn't.

Sleep methods

To help deal with bedtime separation anxiety the Great Ormond Street Children's Hospital in London, UK suggests a parent remains with the baby until she is asleep. Over the next few nights the parent should move further away, but stay in the room until baby is asleep. Eventually the parent should sit outside baby's room, and return quickly if called for, staying for a couple of minutes each time, until baby is asleep.

Then there is the 15-minute method. If a child wakes, the designated parent goes in and comforts her. Parent then leaves. If baby cries again, parent waits for five minutes and then returns to comfort. The wait lengthens five minutes each time to 15, by when baby is asleep.

We're a happy family

SO YOU'VE GOT ONE CHILD, DO YOU WANT ANY MORE? AND WHAT DO YOU WANT TO DO WITH YOUR KIDS? NOW'S THE TIME TO FIGURE OUT STUFF LIKE CRIME AND PUNISHMENT, HOLIDAYS AND SPORT — AND NOT JUST FOR YOU.

How many?

Now that you're at the end of the first year or more of parenting, you should know enough to muddle through for a while. So this section of the book looks ahead and asks you to think about some things you may not have thought about before. It's not all nice, either. To come is a chapter on divorce and another on step-families. It happens. You might not want to consider such a thing now and, of course, you don't have to. Concentrate on this family and making it work.

SO, HOW MANY DO YOU WANT?

You must have discussed it with your partner. There's every chance that you don't agree, but you've started and now you should consider reaching an agreement about this.

If your partner is in her late 30s and you've just had your first child, unless you are considering her being permanently pregnant, there's not much chance of your having four or five kids. Of course, you could have a fertility treatment that has a good

chance of resulting in a multiple birth, but it's probably not a good idea. As a woman gets older there is an increased chance that she will give birth to a disabled child. You have to consider the chances of that happening as time passes and you will have to decide whether you want to raise a disabled or Down's Syndrome child.

You also need to ask yourself if you really want to be attempting to play soccer with a son who's in his teens when you're just about hitting your mid-50s. And on the practical side, if you are in your early to mid-40s when your child is born, you'll be of retirement age when he or she is going through college (and when looking for a job afterwards) and is most likely to need your financial support. Do you want to ask a child in their 20s to care for an elderly parent (you)? It could happen.

ONE

There are plenty of couples out there who opt to have just one child. Those families are perfectly happy, and the child feels special and cared for. As long as the child has friends and family of a similar age, there's no reason why he or she should not enjoy as happy and healthy a childhood as any other. As a parent you have to beware of spoiling the child, of course.

TWO

For many parents, this is the optimum number of offspring. If born with a reasonable age gap – between two and four years, usually – the siblings can become firm friends. Whether the kids are one of each or the same sex, they should be encouraged to form a team and be supportive of each other. Two boys or two girls can save parents money on clothes and toys, of course, while different-sex children don't fight as much over toys or clothes.

THREE

Parents perhaps have to work a little harder in order to create and keep an equitable status quo with three children. But there's no reason why that shouldn't be achievable. Again, the same arguments stand for clothes and toys in regard to the sex of the children.

FOUR

Now you have the makings of a rowing team and can look forward to having a child around your home for a good long while. Obviously it's harder not to make one a favourite child, establishing and maintaining order can be difficult with a majority of one sex over the other (especially if there are more boys) and the toys and clothes argument needs a rethink – they'll be torn, worn out or obsolete by the time the fourth child gets them.

FIVE OR MORE
Why?

Being dad

As your child grows and becomes able to do things without help – from crawling and talking to eating and breaking things – so your relationship with him or her is going to change. How you act and react with your child in the first few years of his or her life is going to have a huge impact on who your child turns out to be. It'll also determine how you turn out to be, too, in your child's memory. So, generally speaking, do you want to be vague, stern, absent or loving? Hoping that you want to be regarded as loving by your children, I can heartily recommend that you learn how to master the Parent/Child Game.

THE PARENT/CHILD GAME

In her book of the same name (1999), British clinical psychologist Sue Jenner sets out the ways in which loving parents can live happily and successfully with their children. The book is clearly and warmly written and contains lots of practical advice and tests, with helpful real-life examples of how certain patterns of behaviour have positively affected families. The fundamental tenet of her book, and of the Parent/Child Game, is that as a parent you must learn how to become child-centred.

BEING CHILD-CENTRED

You may think that you already are child-centred because you pay constant attention to your child. However, being truly, positively child-centred is more than this – it requires a particular kind of attention. It also requires a certain amount of ignoring. Sue Jenner sets out two distinct types of parent–child behaviour:

1 **Child-centred behaviour**
   This means meeting a child's emotional needs or giving them something positive.

2 **Child-directive behaviour**
   This is behaviour that demands a response from the child or tells them what they can or cannot do.

How you act and react with your child in the first few years of his or her life is going to have a huge impact on who your child turns out to be.

Ways in which a parent can be child-centred range from being attentive and commenting positively on what your child is doing, through telling them how great they look in a certain item of clothing, to congratulating them on concentrating well on reading or drawing, and, perhaps most importantly, ignoring minor naughtiness. Jenner also suggests that parents offer praise, smile at their children directly, imitate with enthusiasm noises they make during games, ask them what games to play with them and give positive touches such as hugs and kisses (when the child is receptive and always appropriately).

IGNORING MINOR NAUGHTINESS

This is perhaps the most difficult aspect of the Parent/Child Game. Jenner suggests that you ignore all those little naughty things that your child does, such as picking their nose and eating it, screaming dissent, refusing to wear certain items of clothing, temper tantrums and so on. She offers seven ways to deal with minor naughtiness, among them pretending to be deaf, having a neutral expression, ignoring the child and telling the child that you will only return attention to them when they've stopped the naughty behaviour. In her view, most children under the age of about eight will give up on the naughty behaviour after a minute's ignoring. Good luck.

PRAISING GOOD BEHAVIOUR

Think about it. How much better do you feel when your boss or partner congratulates you on a job or task well done? Now amplify that a hundredfold to get some idea about your child's feelings when you congratulate him or her for doing something well – and it

could be anything at all – from finishing breakfast to reading a book. Gaining parental attention of any emotional colour is the *raison d'être* of all children. So if you don't congratulate them for doing something well, they'll just as likely do it badly in order to get your attention.

On page 174 you'll find advice on how to deal with truly naughty behaviour and ways in which to think about and administer discipline.

How much better do you feel when your boss or partner congratulates you on a job or task well done? Now amplify that a hundredfold to get some idea about your child's feelings when you congratulate him or her for doing something well ...

The child-friendly living room

As your child starts getting around, so he or she will start to explore all of those cupboards and corners that look so fascinating. So you need to decide now whether you mind that sweets are stuffed into your DVD player, that the hi-fi is covered with sticky goo or that the collection of 19th-century pottery is broken. Not that the living room needs to be child-proofed. It can also be made child-friendly.

TELEVISION/HOME ENTERTAINMENT CENTRE
If your TV has to stand on the floor and you can't put it in a cupboard, then establish rules with baby early on. Distract her from the TV by, for example, putting a cloth over it until you want to use it. Watch out for children putting fingers, toys and anything else they can into plug sockets. Always put plug guards in.

WIRING
Most homes have wiring of some sort trailing around: leads for the TV, speaker cable and so on. Try to get it all put under the carpet or floorboards. If that's not feasible then use ties to keep them all together and out of baby's way as much as possible.

CUPBOARDS
Your child is going to be very interested in opening cupboard doors. It's natural. So either get child-proof locks or make sure there's nothing dangerous inside and don't worry that she can open the doors.

SHELVES
Your child is going to want to play wherever you are, so clear the bottom shelves of your things and put hers there instead. Then she won't bother about dull stuff like books that are above her toys and books.

SOFA
Make it a dark colour or cover it with something that you don't mind being ruined.

COFFEE TABLE
At your knee height, a coffee table is just the right size to offer baby something to cling to as she 'walks' around the room. Make sure that it's wood, stable and not precious.

RUG
Don't keep an expensive, collectable or easily damaged rug in your living room. Baby will invariably be sick on it, wipe poo on it or in some other way mark it. Buy a cheap, fun rug that baby can ruin.

TOY TRUNK
If you don't have shelves on which to keep baby's toys and books then get a trunk or storage unit that can hold them.

In the kitchen

While you might think that your child will not spend as much time in the kitchen as the living room, you'd be wrong. Children like to be with their parent wherever, and parents spend a lot of time in the kitchen. So be prepared.

SINK
It's going to be a long time before baby can get into the sink, and by the time she can she won't want to. However, people usually use the cupboard under the sink to keep bleaches and chemical-filled cleaning products. If you don't want the hassle of having to undo a lock every time you want to use these things, try putting them all into a high cupboard.

WASHING MACHINE
Always keep the door closed and the plug socket turned to the 'off' position when not in use. Discourage any attempts by baby to climb in.

DISHWASHER
Always keep the door closed and the plug socket turned to the 'off' position when not in use. Get into the routine of using the dishwasher at night when baby is asleep so that she can't open it mid-wash. Discourage any attempts by baby to climb in.

CUPBOARDS
Your child is going to be very interested in opening cupboard doors. It's natural. So either get child-proof locks, or make sure that there's nothing dangerous inside and don't worry that she can open the doors.

COOKER
It's imperative that your child understands from as early an age as possible that the cooker is hot and not to be touched. You will need to say 'No' a lot. Try to use the back burners as much as possible and never leave anything cooking while you go off and do something else.

TABLE AND CHAIRS
Baby will want to hold on to something to help her stand and 'walk' around. The table and chairs can provide all of that and also be the basis for a great kitchen-based 'den'. Design classics have to be usable here. If you don't want baby goo over the seats or table, don't use them until baby's old enough to know better.

It's playtime

The family that plays together stays together. Playtime is a very important part of family life and you should start getting into it even before your child is a toddler. A child that can play with its parents and not feel afraid of winning or losing but simply enjoy having fun is more likely to grow up feeling secure and happy than a child who doesn't know how to play. So start having fun with your child, but remember that it really isn't about 'winning'.

BABY PLAY

Just because baby can't get around too well yet doesn't mean that you can't play games with her. An early favourite is going to be Peek-A-Boo. You can 'hide' behind your hands or a newspaper for a while, but when she gets bored you'll have to start 'disappearing' behind her chair or cot, behind curtains or doors and so on.

Baby will also love finger puppet shows that take place on her cot side or tabletop. Silly voices are also a must.

You can play physical games with baby, such as pretending to throw her in the air or dancing with her in your arms. Just be aware that those cries that you take for joy could well be fear and if your partner objects to your actions, stop.

You can start swimming with baby at any age, in fact the earlier the better. Not speed crawl or butterfly, of course, but just being in a pool with her will be great fun.

TODDLER PLAY

Now that your child can get around, Hide-and-Seek will be a great favourite, especially if you're pretending to be a child-eating giant while looking for her. Try to ignore her hiding place for as long as possible and look in the most unlikely places, such as the coffee pot, a drawer, a ridiculously high shelf and so on.

Playing catch with a ball (or rolled-up socks) is great for your toddler's hand to eye coordination. Just make sure that the ball is soft enough so that it doesn't hurt when it catches her in the face (and it will). Some parents start their children on tennis at age 3 or so. If you're going to do that, make sure that you get a short junior tennis racquet rather than expecting her to swing your adult-sized one.

By the age of 5 your child should be able to swim pretty well, but before then she can 'swim' with you using floats and armbands.

You can take a jog with your toddler riding her bike alongside, or with you pushing her on a trike.

Toddlers love riding the horsey that dads can become by dropping on all fours and snorting a bit. Be prepared to catch your child as she topples off, usually laughing. Also prepare for the knees of your trousers to wear out faster than at any time since your own childhood.

Some dads like to start gentle rough-housing play at toddler age. Which is fine as long as your child enjoys it, that it's not too close to bedtime and that you are in control of your strength and actions.

CHILD'S PLAY

By the time your child is 7 or more, you should be able to play competitive games with her. The main thing to remember is that you do not teach her anything at all by constantly winning at board games, tennis, soccer or any other such game. If it makes you feel good then you need to see an analyst immediately. There is nothing wrong with your winning at Scrabble occasionally, or beating her in a short race, but it is important that you play her on equal terms. Avoid winning easily at least. It is about the game and spending time with your child, not about winning and losing.

... you do not teach her anything at all by constantly winning at board games, tennis, soccer or any other such game.

6

Crime and punishment

As Raskolnikov would tell you, guilt is a terrible thing. It makes people do terrible things and affects us all in a terrible way. The father who snaps at his child, the father who ignores his child and even the father who beats his child are all guilt-ridden, and so they should be. The role of a parent carries an enormous responsibility. As an adult you have the power to determine what a 'crime' in your home is and what 'punishment' fits the 'crime'. If you are one of those sad and desperate fathers who love this part of parenting then there's every chance that your own father was strict with you, and probably beat you for 'doing wrong'. Well, now is your chance to stop a nasty pattern repeating itself.

SET THE RULES

There seems to be an increasing number of parents who believe not only that smacking your child is wrong, but that teaching their children how to behave politely and generously is also wrong. Somehow they seem to think that a child knows best how to behave, from when and what to eat, to when to go to bed and how to take what they want, whenever they want it. Parents who believe that they are being 'liberal' and allowing their children's 'natural character' to emerge are simply wrong.

Often parents who think that they are being 'liberal' with their children have suffered from an overly strict upbringing themselves. Others allow their children to act without boundaries because they feel guilty about the lack of parental care that they have been able to give their children. Working

Spare the rod

In many enlightened countries it is illegal for a parent to beat a child. It is illegal to even smack the child. If you happen to live in a country where it isn't illegal, just pretend that it is. If you were beaten as a kid, ask yourself, did you enjoy it? Do you love your father because of it? Anyone who answers 'Yes' is in serious denial.

It is not acceptable for a father to hit, smack or beat his children. Never. If you lose your temper and hit out (at anyone, let alone your family), you have to accept the guilt that goes with that action and reaction and admit that you are a failure. If you want to continue to be a failure, carry on lashing out. If you want to get over it, however, seek professional help.

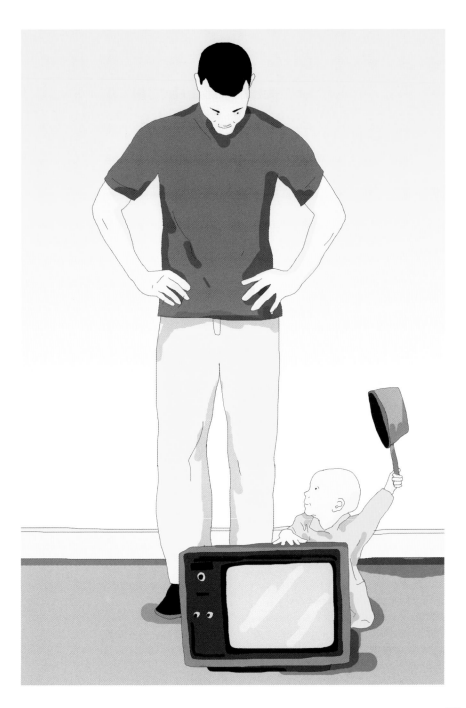

If you ignore the small stuff, you'll find that when it comes to the big stuff – hurting a sibling or friend, say – your command or stating 'No' has more effect.

parents who have put their offspring into nursery or day-care since they were 3 months old, for example, may encourage children to be 'free' to compensate for the strictures of that early experience.

This is all wrong. A child needs to know its boundaries. If a child is 'naturally rebellious', then unless that child knows what to rebel against, that 'natural' character is going to remain suppressed, or become warped.

There is every reason for you as a father to set rules for your children, from being polite to eating properly at a dining table, saying 'please' and 'thank you' and not taking things away from other children because they can.

DON'T JUST SAY 'NO'
The Parent/Child Game (see page 166) provides a pretty good way for you to set boundaries without being overly authoritarian, angry or demanding of your children. If you follow the Ignoring Minor Naughtiness rules as set out earlier, you will find that the minor naughtiness decreases. That's all very well, but how to deal with the major naughtiness?

Well, if you are more child-centred than child-directive, you may just find that there isn't very much major naughtiness to deal with. As Sue Jenner points out, adults often make hundreds of redundant orders to their children every day – most of which involve the child being told not to do something or other which, really, isn't that bad or dangerous. If you ignore the small stuff, you'll find that when it comes to the big stuff – hurting a sibling or friend, say – your command or stating 'No' has more effect. It can be very difficult to start ignoring minor naughtiness, but it's worth persevering. See The Parent/Child Game for full instructions on how to make it work.

DO JUST SAY 'NO'
There are of course times when you have to command your children to stop. Venturing close to things that could endanger them, such as traffic, cliff edges, fire, falling trees etc., will result in an almost involuntary shout from you of 'No!' or 'Stop!' And so it should. There may be times when you have to physically remove your child from a situation (a fight, say). It should be done firmly, not violently. A smack is still out of the question.

DEALING WITH AN AGGRESSIVE CHILD

If your child is physically or verbally aggressive towards you, other members of the family or friends, then you have to ask yourself why this is. It is very likely that your child is trying to tell you something that she doesn't have the vocabulary for. She could be repeating behaviour she's witnessed elsewhere. She could be reacting instinctively because she feels angry and ignored. All of which you need to discover and set right. If your child is hitting you, then hold her tight in a smothering embrace, talk calmly and gently and tell her that you love her. Do not strike back, send her to her room or laugh at her. You need to find out what is troubling her. (Of course it's a big subject, and if you have a seriously aggressive child you will need to seek professional help.)

BE CONSISTENT

It's imperative that whatever strategy you adopt in regard to discipline you have the full agreement of your partner. And that both of you are consistent about it. If one parent is ignoring minor naughtiness and the other is still telling the child to stop all of the time, then the child will naturally become confused. Worse, the child is likely to favour being with the parent who ignores the minor naughtiness, thus setting in motion a common and destructive chain of argument and playing off one parent against the other.

PS ...

Could all of you supposedly 'liberal' parents out there reading this ask yourselves if you like the fact that the world is forgetting all about manners and how to be civil? If you want people to be polite to each other and to you, if you want more considerate and responsible action in society, then start teaching your children how and why such things are important. Don't be so lazy as to think that school will teach them, because it won't.

Other people's children

Some very wise guy once said that hell is other people's children. And he had a point. No matter what you do to teach your own children good manners, politeness and consideration towards others, there will always be other people's children ready to teach them the opposite.

HOW TO CHOOSE FRIENDS FOR YOUR CHILD

You don't. No matter how much you might want your child to be best friends with the children of your own best friend, they will always make pals with whoever they feel happiest with. You cannot match-make friends with kids, so don't try. Up to early pre-teen years you might find that your child will happily get along with other children that you put them into contact with – on the occasion of a visit of old friends with kids the same age, for example. But at school and in their own life (and that's what their school days represent – their own lives), your child will hang out with who they want to.

WHAT TO DO IF THEIR FRIENDS ARE 'A BAD INFLUENCE'

Never try to influence your child into disliking their friends. The more that you decry the friend as a 'bad influence' the more intrigued by them your child will become. Encourage your child to bring their friend home with them to your house. Then treat the friend as if they are one of your own children. After all, if the friend has chosen to spend time with your beautifully behaved, polite and considerate child, they must see something there that they like. Possibly they want to be like your child, so encourage that.

WHAT TO DO IF YOUR FRIEND'S CHILDREN ARE HELL

There is every chance that you and/or your partner have pals who want to be 'liberal' parents and do not give their children parameters in their lives. Which means that your friends' children are hellish brats who do not know the words 'please' or 'thank you'. There's a good chance that your children will not want to play with theirs. There should also be a good chance that you do not consider them to be such close friends any more. It happens. If these friends of yours are not so close to you that you are able to tell them that your kids don't like playing with theirs (and why), then the friendship will necessarily fade away. You'll probably have to turn down a few invitations to their place before they get the message, but they will, eventually.

Some very wise guy once said that hell is other people's children.

When the children of family go bad

Unlike the previous scenario with friends, hopefully there will be less of a problem with telling family that you don't agree with the way their children are behaving. Although there probably will be the same problems. In which case, if family gatherings happen at your home, and the children of siblings or in-laws are behaving badly, it is your prerogative to treat them like your own children:

Make them say 'please' and 'thank you'.

Make them sit at the dinner table until everyone is finished.

Make them eat what your children eat (no dipping into cereal because they don't like 'grown-up' food).

Do not smack them, as much as you may want to.

Deny them access to sharp knives and shout 'No!' at them as they attempt to decapitate the family cat or dog.

Be prepared for a family argument as their parents accuse you of being too strict with your children.

If you are able to tell them that their kids are brats but they still don't want to do anything about it, then you won't be socializing as families any more. You can still socialize as adults. Though why you'd want to is beyond me. If you are able to be honest and the friends seem to take notice then good, you may have helped them greatly.

Holidays in the sun

Unlike holidaying with a baby (see page 157), going on holiday with a walking, talking child or children is a matter of pleasing the kids, not just you. While you could trek over the Andes with baby in a sling on your back, attempting to push or drag school-age kids over mountains is not easy and certainly not fun. So prepare yourself for a couple of weeks in the sun instead, relaxing and having fun with the kids. Of course, if you're an active family who are all skilled in white-water rafting or can happily sail down the Amazon in a gondola, you won't need to read this stuff.

WHERE TO?

Your summer holiday destinations are now going to require certain absolutes. Firstly,

Holidaying with other families – the etiquette

If you are planning on taking a holiday with another family, there are a few things to consider.

Your children and theirs have to get along well. If your friends' kids are brats, don't go.

You have to agree with your friends' parenting methods.

Agree to share all shopping, cooking, cleaning and babysitting duties equally, before you go. And stick to it. Also agree to equally share all expenses.

Be aware of your friends' family dietary requirements – it would be awful for only one family to be vegetarian, for instance.

If you don't know the family that you plan to take a long holiday with very well, take a short break together first, to see if you get on.

Book (or take) two vehicles so that each family can get away independently of each other.

If you remember all of the essential items you'll need and you've done the groundwork to ensure that you'll have fun with whoever you're going on holiday with, you should enjoy a stress-free holiday!

Packing checklist

| The children's passports as well as yours (if travelling abroad, obviously).

| The children's necessary beach (or other) equipment, such as buckets, spades, swimsuits, armbands (if needed) and inflatable toys.

| Any of the children's comfort items, such as blankets, soft toys or anything else that they 'can't sleep without'.

| Wet-weather entertainment, including videos or DVDs (if the place you will be staying in has the necessary equipment), hand-held computer game consoles, books, board games, toys or writing and colouring books with crayons, etc.

| Any essential food items that may not be easily bought where you're going but which are allowed to be taken into the country: Marmite, for instance.

there has to be sun, sand and water. If you're staying in a hotel the rooms must interconnect. If you're in a rented house, cabin or villa there must be a pool, or be within walking distance of the beach. And that walking distance should not have to cross a road. Your holiday accommodation should offer enough space for everyone to spread out, and if there is a threat of bad weather, wherever you're staying must have a TV with satellite access, a video or DVD player and all must be in working condition.

You'll want a child-friendly restaurant within easy reach. Oh, and there has to be low risk of kidnap or robbery by bandits or terrorists. If holidaying abroad, there has to be a stable and benign government in power.

ALONE AGAIN, OR NOT?

There are several reasons for your family not to take a holiday alone. The best one being that, if there are more adults than children, then you, the parents, are more likely to be able to find time to have a break yourselves. Holidaying with family is good – grandparents or aunts and uncles always like to spend time with their grandchildren/nieces and nephews. You can take a few afternoons or evenings off while they babysit. Don't push it, though: two or maybe three a week is the tops. After all, you're there to holiday as a family.

If you're travelling with friends who also have kids (see opposite), you can organize babysitting schedules, preferably before you go. Again, no more than twice a week.

Teenage Kicks

THESE ARE THE DIFFICULT YEARS. HOPEFULLY YOU'LL REMEMBER YOUR
OWN TEENAGE LIFE AND GO EASY ON YOUR KIDS. PERSONALLY, I THINK
THAT YOU SHOULD ACCEPT THAT YOUR TEENAGERS ARE GOING TO HAVE
SEX AND EXPERIMENT WITH DRUGS AT SOME STAGE. SO MAKE IT SAFE
FOR THEM BY LETTING THEM DO IT AT HOME, WHERE YOU CAN BE ON
HAND TO HELP IF NEEDED.

A space of their own

HIS PRE-TEEN BEDROOM
(see page 184)

HER PRE-TEEN BEDROOM
(see page 188)

HIS TEENAGE BEDROOM
(see page 186)

HER TEENAGE BEDROOM
(see page 190)

His pre-teen bedroom

Up until his 13th birthday, your son will be a generally uncomplicated soul. His bedroom will reflect that. He'll have his obsessions – usually sports- or game-related – which are represented in his room by posters, equipment, clothing. There'll be a lot of toys still remaining from his early years. There may be models, train or car track set-ups, things attached to the ceiling. Maybe he has an interest in astronomy, or biology, shown by star charts and globes, a human-sized skeleton that glows in the dark. His bed will be covered with a duvet that reflects his interest in either a sports star or comic book hero. There will be a desk with a computer on it and his homework scattered across it. A telescope at the window points at the sky. This is his world. Over the page you will find a facsimile of this world as it has progressed through his teenage years. It is not a pretty sight.

His teenage bedroom

Sometime around your son's 13th birthday, he'll change. No longer will he babble on excitedly about a new video game, sports star or TV programme. Instead, he will grunt and moan, 'I hate you'. His clothes will become too baggy. His jeans will look as if they're falling down all of the time. He'll look as if he's stopped washing his hair, but will always smell of aftershave. His room has changed, too. Now his computer is painted black, he has acquired a TV set and a stereo system (both black). He has painted his room shades of black and red. The sports stars have been replaced by bands with names like Blood, Dirt and Murder. There is a graphic anti-vivisection poster featuring a smoking beagle. The overhead light no longer works, and his lamps are covered with cloth. Candles burn in wine bottles. The door has a skull and crossbones painted on it in blood red, and a 'NO ENTRY' sign is placed at a prominent angle. The telescope now points at a house across the street where you know that a 16-year-old girl lives. His globe has been painted with swastikas on America and Africa is covered in blood clots. Everything in his clothes closet is black or red. Black sneakers and biker boots litter the floor. His bookcase is almost obliterated by a guitar amplifier and a black bass guitar.

Her pre-teen bedroom

If you live in a city, you will notice your daughter taking an interest in fashion, boys, make-up, boy pop stars and actors from the age of 9 or so. If you don't live in a city you might witness your daughter clinging to her childish interests – animals, cuddly toys, dressing up in Disney princess outfits – until she's about 11 years old. Which is not just another way of saying you should desert the inner city for the country or a small town, although it's as good a reason as any. For girls, who mature earlier than boys, what previous generations might have termed the teen years in reality begin earlier. Parents find themselves feeling nostalgic for those pre-teen years as their growing daughters show ever more precocity. So, enjoy your daughter's pre-teen bedroom while you can.

Her teenage bedroom

After your daughter's 12th birthday, she'll start asking that you knock and wait for her to invite you in to her room. She'll also have asked by now to redecorate. The pony and teddy bear posters will have been replaced by boy pop stars and actors. She will have demanded a dressing table, which is full of make-up. The curtains will be replaced by sheer sheets of gossamer and a venetian blind. The floor will be covered with cushions and bean bags, necessary since her bedroom (now referred to only as her 'room') has become the chosen meeting place for her gang of female friends and, increasingly, boys.

When to worry

As a parent you are always going to worry about your children. It's only natural. However, as your offspring reach their teenage years and start trying out the idea that they are going to lead separate and independent lives, one in which you play less of a central role, you are going to worry more. It is pointless for anyone to tell you not to worry, because there will be a constant, low-level buzz of worry permanently going on in your head. You'll grow accustomed to it, you may even get to ignore it. However, there may be times when ignoring it is not the best course of action.

DON'T WORRY WHEN

- Your teenager starts going to bed late and sleeping later.

- Your teenager starts changing friends at an alarming rate.

- Your teenager doesn't want to do the things with you that you thought you all enjoyed – like going on holiday, visiting grandparents or having an Indian meal.

- The telephone rings and when you answer there's no one there – it'll be a tongue-tied girl or boy looking for your son or daughter and too embarrassed to talk to you.

- Your son refuses to go to the game with you.

- Your daughter refuses to go shopping with you.

- The level on your vodka goes down faster than you remember drinking it, or beers start disappearing from the fridge.

- You're sure you can smell cigarette smoke in the house even though no one in the family smokes (you think).

- You feel like blurting, 'You're not going out like that!'

- Your teenager starts debating politics with you and accuses you of being a fascist.

- Your music collection starts getting mixed up and missing elements turn up all over the house.

- That antique leather jacket that you'd hung on to since you were 22 has gone from your closet.

- You feel like shouting, 'Turn that racket down!'

DO WORRY WHEN
- The local police automatically know where to bring your comatose teenager.

- The phone rings and you are too scared to answer it.

- You call your teenager's school to ask about parent-teacher evenings and they say, 'Who?'

REWARD! REWARD! REWARD!

WANTED

Ask gramps

Because we all have a selective memory when it comes to our own past failings, you might want to ask your father what you were like as a teenager. You might be surprised to hear that you were not the suave, collected, stylish individual that you recall. If your father has any photographs to back up his memory of your appalling dress sense and behaviour, take a look at them. You should also share this evidence of your own teen failings with your children. It'll help keep the hypocrisy out of your commands to them.

- Your car is forever being 'stolen'.

- You bump into the guy that you buy your monthly supply of dope from coming out of your teenager's bedroom.

- Your daughter's boyfriends all seem to be your age.

- Your son's girlfriends all seem to dress like hookers.

- You regularly have to face charges relating to antisocial behaviour.

- Your teenager is forever calling you a deadbeat and has a personal assistant, lawyer and accountant.

- Your teenager asks to be sent to a boarding school or military academy.

- You begin to see your teenager only on local news reports.

- Your son keeps trying to engage you in conversation about assault rifles.

- There are a bunch of strangers regularly having breakfast with you.

CONCLUSION

Your biggest worry should be that your teenage offspring begin to drift away from the family. You will inevitably spend less time with them, but they must know you are always there when they do want to talk. You should know and trust their circle of friends – and that includes their friends' parents. Offer inclusion in everything that you do, but don't push them to be involved; they must want to.

Live fast, die young

If you find this heading brutal and scary, then good. It's meant to shock you. As an adult you are all too aware of how precious life is and how easily it can be lost or ruined by the dumbest act. If you are not, then grow up. Your teenage son or daughter is probably not yet aware of how fragile life can be. Having been protected and sheltered from the potential dangers of adult life, they are now going to come face to face with what can be a disturbing reality. It's your duty as a parent to help them to understand and deal with some of the more difficult aspects of their teenage years.

EAT ME

Hopefully you are aware of the benefits of a healthy relationship with food and have brought up your children to eat well. The more meals that you eat together as a family, the better, especially home-cooked ones (and I know I'm repeating myself, but with some things repetition is required). Combine eating well with a physically active life and you'll have a good recipe for instilling a healthy relationship with food in your teenage children.

Kids get fat not just because they eat food full of fat, but also because they don't exercise. If your child's school does not provide enough physical activity during the week, you should encourage it out of school hours. Boys can play football or other ball games and often do, which is perhaps one reason why they suffer fewer eating disorders than girls. Getting a daughter interested in sport is perhaps not as easy but is possibly more important. Try tennis,

cycling, swimming, hockey or soccer. If you have the chance, take your daughter sailing or to play golf with you (or whatever sport that you enjoy) at as young an age as you can. Small children grow up believing that any activity they undertake from a young age is 'normal' and will not think twice about carrying on with it as they grow up.

There's every chance, though, that even if you have never taken them to a fast-food restaurant, your teenagers will eat a burger, fries and milkshake in a burger chain at some point. That's fine, don't worry about it. It's not the odd burger or milkshake that is the problem in itself, but the health and obesity problems that can follow and, particularly for girls, what this can do to their self-image. In the UK some 20% of children under the age of 15 are obese. Anorexia is rife in Western societies. Having brought up a daughter to eat the right kinds of food – organic, rich in vitamins and fibre etc. – is no guarantee that she will not turn to unhealthy eating patterns as a teenager, unfortunately.

It does make it more unlikely, though, especially given that you as a parent are likely to be more involved in your child's life.

WHAT TO DO IF YOUR DAUGHTER IS 'TOO FAT'

Talk to her as an equal. Come up with practical and healthy ways in which you can make her feel good about herself. If there is a genuine need for weight loss, make sure that she loses weight safely. Ask a GP for help if necessary. DO NOT attempt to laugh off her fears about being overweight or patronize her about them.

SEX AND DRUGS AND ROCK AND ROLL

When the inventive British singer-songwriter Ian Dury came up with his song of the same name in 1977 it was considered outrageous (it's chorus reckons that sex and drugs and rock and roll are all a body needs) and morally reprehensible. Today it seems as quaint as those 1940s music-hall songs that Max Miller did in 1977. If the 1960s were the dawn of the age of permissiveness, the beginning of the 21st century seems to be the wee small hours of the same age.

SEX

With the increase in hormones racing around a teenager's body, growth spurts and changes in their psychological and sexual persona it's no wonder they go a little 'mad'. The awakening of a libido is a powerful driving force in both boys and girls. It can also be frightening for them. It is important that your children have the proper understanding of what sex is, and you cannot expect their school to teach them the facts of life.

The figures on teenage sexual activity are frightening. The UK and US have the highest rates of teenage pregnancy in the developed

Sexually transmitted disease among teens has grown threefold in 6 years …

world. Sexually transmitted diseases (STDs) among teens has grown threefold in six years, with the potentially permanently damaging chlamydia being especially infectious (it can cause infertility in girls). All of this despite the ever-present threat of AIDs, and in the face of almost universal awareness of the benefits and availability of condoms to young people.

The time when a father had only to worry about his son getting a girl pregnant or his daughter becoming pregnant seems almost like a golden age of parental worry. Today you have to worry about your son's possible involvement in gang rape (another extremely worrying trend over the past few years among teenagers), his contracting a STD and developing a wholly unacceptable attitude towards women as well as his becoming a teenage father. You have to worry about the same things with your daughter, too.

Do not refuse to talk to them about anything, and when you do talk, treat them as an equal, not a child.

Do not ignore the tell-tale signs that your child is interested in sex and hope that they'll get over it.

Do not ban them from having a boyfriend or girlfriend in their bedroom, alone. It's going to be much safer for your children to have sexual experiences in your home than it is on the street or in any other place you'd really rather not know about.

As with most things connected to your children's teenage years, the preventive work needs to begin long before they reach age 13. The biggest single weapon your children will hold against becoming involved in unsavoury and dangerous sexual behaviour is self-respect. If you can instil in your children the idea that the kind of boorish behaviour advocated by crass movies, morally objectionable pop songs and videos and teen magazines is somehow pathetic and beneath their contempt, so much the better. Making

both sexes respect the other from an early age will help. Openly ridiculing the objectification of women as practised by lads' mags will work against you with your son, but being honest and open with your partner and daughter in front of your son, and suggesting that this is behaviour worth following, may well work.

Likewise, your daughter should feel proud to follow the example of her mother – who, being your partner and emotional and economic equal, is a perfect female role model. It is increasingly difficult to build a belief in self-worth when your children are witnessing the deification of individuals by the media for the simple fact of their taking

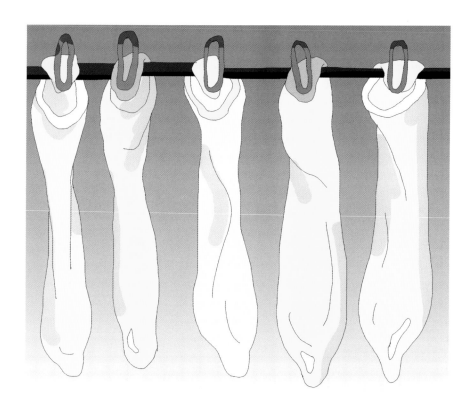

7

their clothes off or having a nice smile, but you have to try. Point your children towards media that appreciate and celebrate equality of the sexes and self-respect. Sit on the sofa with them on a wet Sunday afternoon and watch *His Girl Friday* (you might have to explain some of the jokes). Give them a copy of Sartre's *Age of Reason* on their 15th birthday. Look back to what made you the man that you are (or want to be) and pass on some age-old wisdom. Most importantly, accept that your teenage son or daughter is going to be experimenting with sex. Make it as easy for them to do it in a responsible manner as you can.

DRUGS

All the statistics point to the probability that your teenage offspring are going to be either drunk or stoned before their 15th birthday, and quite likely both. In the highly improbable event that you have been neither drunk nor stoned in your life, you have to take my word for it that it doesn't matter. Neither alcohol nor, increasingly, cannabis is illegal. They are both easy to get hold of (you will have alcohol in the house and maybe even dope) and they don't have lasting side-effects. And despite what Reefer Madness might say, neither is addictive, nor do they lead to heroin addiction. That is, unless your son or daughter is inclined towards it.

... you simply have to accept that your teenager is going to get drunk and smoke dope.

Collect proof before acting. Do not confront them and create tension unnecessarily. Do not ask why they are doing it. They won't know and the problem is likely to be you anyway. Seek professional help. Don't think that it's a passing phase and forget about it.

This may sound blasé, even unhelpful to some of you, but you simply have to accept that your teenager is going to get drunk and smoke dope. They may even experiment with other drugs, like speed (amphetamine), Ecstasy, LSD and cocaine. If, however, they have had the right kind of happy and healthy upbringing and enjoy a stable relationship with their parents, they are highly unlikely to become addicted to any of those substances. In fact, it's easier to become an alcoholic.

If, however, they are unhappy at home, or have any other serious problems, and have friends who have regular access to hard (class A) drugs that include crack cocaine and heroin, then you have to worry.

Do not worry about finding cannabis in their room or smelling it on them.

Do not ask who their dealer is and see if they can get some for you. It will embarrass them and they'll lose respect for you.

Do not boast about your youthful drinking excesses and don't offer cautionary tales about your drinking or drug-taking past.

Do not be judgemental if your teenager begins to tell you about their drinking or drug-taking; be neutral.

Do not judge or otherwise condemn any of their friends that you know (or think that you know) are either drinking too heavily or taking too many drugs.

Encourage responsible drinking and remind them that smoking is bad for their health, regardless of what's in the roll-up. As with the question of sex and eating habits, all of the hard work needed to prevent your children from overdoing the drinking and drug-taking in their teenage years is actually done in the preceding years. There's no need, for example, to refuse your child a taste of wine, regardless of their age. Usually they'll hate it and it will remove any curiosity that they might otherwise have had. Don't smoke when you think they won't know – children always know. When they ask you about smoking put your case simply and effectively – but strongly. Saying that you don't like the taste won't do it. Telling them that it can kill you will. There's nothing wrong with a shock for your kids sometimes.

ROCK 'N' ROLL

Give it up. At your age it's unseemly to try to impress your teenagers with your hoary tales of a rock 'n' roll past. They won't care and won't understand your delight at seeing Genesis in a wet field in 1975, Peter Frampton in a stadium in 1979, Queen anywhere in 1984 or even Nirvana at a small club in 1991. Don't force your musical tastes on them; let them discover their own, if they want to. And certainly don't complain that what your teenagers choose to listen to is rubbish. You're turning into your dad.

Don't be a cool dad

Despite what various men's mags and adverts hoping to sell you stuff might say, there is no such thing as a cool dad. To a teenager a dad is simply that. If you've done a half-decent job up to this point, then your teenager might just tolerate your being around and even talk to you occasionally. They will certainly appreciate your being there to give them money, a lift or an argument when they feel like it. But most importantly, and they will not know how to say this, they will love you and need you to be a dad. They will not need you to be a pal, a mate, a friend. They will have lots of those and they'll all be their own age. They will be embarrassed enough by you without your trying to chat about music, clothes, games or films. It might be hard, but accept that you are not a teenager and therefore are incapable of being 'cool'.

We're not a happy family

ACCORDING TO SOME HALF-QUALIFIED GEEK, BEING A COMMUTER IS
MORE STRESSFUL THAN BEING A FIGHTER JET PILOT. SO WHERE DOES
THAT PLACE THE STRESS LEVEL FOR A MAN WHO'S CONSTANTLY
ARGUING WITH HIS WIFE AND KIDS? IT HAPPENS AND OFTEN. FAMILIES
CAN SPLIT ALL TOO EASILY. TRY YOUR DAMNEDEST NOT TO, BUT IF YOU
MUST THEN DIVORCE YOUR LOVED ONES WITH DIGNITY.

Parent trouble

8

Unless you are the 3-D equivalent of the Flanders family in *The Simpsons*, at times there are going to be problems in your relationship with your partner and with your children. If you are reading this before you have become a father, you probably don't want to read the following, but it's worth taking note and thinking about. If you are reading this because things haven't been going quite as well as you'd hoped since becoming a dad, then hopefully the next few pages will go some way to making yours a happy family once more.

THINK

Since the birth of your child, you will have been involved in building and maintaining a family from a wholly new position. As a child and living at home you were part of a family unit and the memory of that, combined with the memory of your parents' relationship, has informed your behaviour as a father. Which of course is fine if your father and mother had a good relationship and both parents were around as you grew up. However, while there is statistically a good chance that your parents were together for most of your childhood, there is less chance that you will remain a solid family unit until your child is an adult. Times, unfortunately, have changed.

So think about it. Do you want your family unit to fall apart? Is it really all someone else's fault and are you ready to quit now? You may well be carrying a long list of grievances against your partner, but you have to ask yourself if they are all real (and fair). Some men even blame the child or children for the collapse of an adult relationship. Which, when you think about it, is pretty ridiculous. How can a small child be responsible for your problems when you are supposed to be taking care of theirs?

If you are feeling trapped, unable to see a future for you and your partner and wishing that things could be just like they were before becoming a dad, you need to go right back to the beginning of this book and take that long look in the mirror.

Oh, and in case you still don't get it, here it is spelt out. G.E.T. O.V.E.R. I.T. Put another way it spells: Grow Up.

HOW TO AVOID PROBLEMS IN YOUR MARRIAGE

The focus of this book has been on your becoming a half-decent father and predominantly on your relationship with your child. If at times it has been assumed that your relationship with your partner is fine and healthy, that was a hopeful assumption. While you and your partner will have to accept that you can each take a certain amount of love and support from each other for granted, the relationship will still need work.

- Love your partner. You should remind yourself that you do love her as often as once a week. And you should tell her that just as often. Simply hearing the words spoken can mean a lot.

- Resist the temptation to bitch about your partner, and certainly resist the urge to ever tell anyone that she doesn't understand you – except her. By all means discuss any marital problems that you might feel strongly about with a good friend or professional, just don't use it as a prop in relationship-building with others.

- Talk openly and honestly with your partner about anything that bothers you. Make sure that any conversations take place at the right time and in the right mood. Don't accuse her of anything, don't shout and do listen to what she has to say in response.

- If you can possibly manage it, make sure that you and your partner have a regular night out together. It could be as often as once a week or once a month, but you should certainly make time to be yourselves without having to think about the children. On that night out, make it a rule not to discuss the children unless you really have to. Also try not to moan about work (either of you). If you have trouble in finding subjects that don't concern the

How can a small child be responsible for your problems when you are supposed to be taking care of theirs?

kids or work to talk about, go to see a movie, or a concert, something that means you can be together without having to talk.

SATURDAY NIGHT'S NOT ALL RIGHT FOR FIGHTING

Tensions between parents will always affect the children. However, the occasional shouting match between you is not going to turn them into trembling wrecks. If you and your partner are prone to volatile displays of emotion and always have been, it's not necessary for either or both of you to be put on a course of downers for the sake of the children. As long as you are both aware of the other's tendency to explode occasionally, and don't let it alter your relationship or cloud your true feelings for one another, then it shouldn't have an adverse effect upon your children. Of course it's not a great example to set them and you shouldn't get angry with them if they begin to have tantrums over the slightest thing. After all, it's what they're used to, isn't it? But bottling things up all the time is not particularly helpful.

Having said that (and hopefully it's sunk in), there is absolutely no reason for you or your partner to bully each other or the children. You know that physical violence – a

Consistency, consistency, consistency

It's one of the great secrets of raising kids and of marriage maintenance, too. Since you have to improvise with kids as new situations arise, and you have to set new rules that you hadn't imagined before encountering such a situation, you necessarily have to communicate with your partner to pass on such edicts as they are issued. The very fact of your communicating with your partner, even on small matters (how many cookies are they allowed a day? Can they go to little Johnny's house more than three times a week?) is a boon to your relationship. Of course you need consistency in your relationship with your partner, too. And that can best be served by your continually communicating with each other and trusting one another.

ANGER MANAGEMENT

If, as is to be hoped, you have managed to control your temper when confronted by the infuriating behaviour of your child and you have not hit or otherwise physically handled them, then you could well be feeling pent up. It's all too easy to take this built-up anger out on your partner. Or while driving, or at work – usually making an inferior quake in their boots. None of which is to be recommended. As previously suggested, perhaps you should have a physical activity that helps you to channel your anger in positive ways. If you have a real problem with controlling anger – and are increasingly finding that counting to ten before responding to a demanding child, or leaving the house after an 'incident' to shout or run it off, is not solving the problem – then you should seek professional help.

WHOSE SIDE ARE YOU ON?

Do not even think about uttering this phrase to your children. No matter what the temptation is, do not ever ask your children to take sides in arguments between you and their mother. Not even in fun. Children cannot make such a choice. It's too confusing for them and will only create anxiety and uncertainty. Using a child as a weapon in adult war games is cowardly and will ultimately damage your relationship with the child, as well as with your partner.

smack or a push counts – is forbidden and dumb. So, too, are relentless haranguing, shouting and demanding from parents. Not at the kids and not at each other. If drinking makes either of you worse, don't drink. And certainly don't think that just because the children are in bed you can shout at each other, either. They can hear. Remember your own childhood.

And certainly don't think that just because the children are in bed you can shout at each other, either. They can hear.

D.I.V.O.R.C.E.

Stands for Don't If Very Or Relatively Confused Enter.

Getting a divorce has to be the last resort, and not just for the sake of the children, although they will always suffer, no matter how 'amicable' any divorce is. For your own sake, try everything that you can before ending your marriage and rupturing your family. Of course, if you started your marriage in anything but a totally committed state of mind, you'll probably regard the legal end of your marriage as just another stage of life and the door through which you can get on with the rest of your life. If you think that, then bully for you, dumbwit. Once you have children there is no thinking about the rest of just your life; you have theirs to consider, too. Which is why, if you really have to divorce, you need to make it as painless for everyone as possible.

ARE YOU SURE?

Unfortunately, many marriages fall apart within two years of the birth of the first child and a great number that survive that time period can fail within two years of the birth of a second child. It's a hard time for the parents' relationship. The mother's attention can be predominantly upon the child or children while a working father can spend increasingly less time with his family in order to earn enough money to feed a growing household. If the mother also works full-time, then both parents will be tired and frequently absent from each other, meaning that they have to cram all of their time together into weekends. It's never a perfect arrangement and full of potentially fatal strains on your marriage.

If you're valued at your work, they'll try to accommodate any working patterns that you might suggest. If you're not valued, why work there?

So ask yourself...

What's the most important thing in your life? Is it your job, status, car or bank account? Or is it the love and support of your family?

Sociologists, psychologists and family 'experts' have for some time and will continue to present statistics that show how in most families in the Western world, the father is the principal bread-winner and the mother spends more time with the children. Divorce statistics will invariably point to men having far less contact with their children after the split. When questioned, men will claim that they have to work too hard – in order to pay the family support and allow them to live their own (separate) lives – to be able to see their children.

Are you heading that way?

Are you hiding from your family life by assuming that work is more important? It's an easy excuse - and one of the more acceptable – for fathers not to participate in family life. It can start off being the reason why difficulties arise in your relationship with your partner in the first place and can easily become the reason why divorce might be suggested. Men like to complain about a Catch-22 situation where they have to work in order to pay for family life but the pressure of that work means that they can't enjoy time with their family. Does that sound familiar?

If it does then:

Change your working life ...

GET A NEW JOB

If you really do care about your marriage and family, and you know that it's your work causing all of your problems, then change your job. Oh yes, you think, it's very easy to say that when you're sitting at home writing this drivel and being paid for it, what about me with my office job, company car and huge mortgage to pay? I can't interface with IT (or whatever other boring work you do) from home, can I?

Really? You can't? Have you asked your boss about working flexi hours, doing stuff from home? If you're valued at your work, they'll try to accommodate any working patterns that you might suggest. If you're not valued, why work there?

If your company refuses to be accommodating and there's no way that you can do fewer hours in the office or work from home, get a new job, one that does allow you to spend more time with your family. And if you can't get another job that easily, how about your partner working? You could move house and have a smaller mortgage and better quality of life if you both worked different hours. Learn to live with fewer material goods and still be happy.

DON'T GET A NEW JOB

It's OK, I'm not a 'good-life Nazi'. Not everyone can or wants to chuck in their job and move somewhere more pleasant to live than a traffic-laden, grimy, tense inner city. I know that. So work fewer hours (check your contract) and shift your focus from pleasing the boss to pleasing your family. Get your employer to provide you with a laptop so you can leave early and put in the last hour of your working day on the train. Or work a compressed week. Modern technology means that so much can be done remotely. Take advantage of it. A job should only ever be a means to an end, not the living end.

If you must

If it really is impossible for you to keep the marriage together, then you should try to make the proceedings as painless as possible. Just because you and your partner no longer feel that you can share a bed and much of a life together it doesn't mean that the family unit has to split up. Just the opposite. You should try to keep the family unit as intact as possible.

SEPARATE

Many children are afraid of the word divorce, let alone the reality. Separation doesn't seem quite as final, somehow. It's also a lot cheaper, of course. If you and your partner are still friends and there isn't 'anyone else' for either of you, then you can even legally separate and continue to live in the family home. As long as you don't sleep in the same

bed, eat meals together or otherwise share domestic chores – you doing her washing or ironing, for instance – then in the eyes of the law, you are separated. Of course, if you are not considering further legal action concerning your marriage, such as an eventual divorce, you don't need to consider what is legally binding during a separation.

The children will (hopefully) hardly notice any difference at home. Unless you've bumped one of them out of their own room and into sharing with a sibling so that you can sleep in their room, of course.

You don't need any paperwork when you separate, although if you do both sign a deed of separation it can be useful if and when you need to sort out tax or government benefits. It can also be useful if or when you do come to divorce. In the UK a divorce is easy to obtain if you've been separated for two years and while a court has limited power to make judgements on financial or child-related matters, anything that you agree while separated can be a useful basis for the terms of the divorce. So make sure that you agree on what financial support both of you are going to make to the family. Home ownership is a potentially difficult affair, but if you are being cordial and agreeable about everything else, there's no reason why you shouldn't agree on whether to sell the house, and how to split the proceeds if you do.

DIVORCE WITHOUT RANCOUR

You do not need to see a solicitor to get a divorce. There are websites from which you can download the relevant forms, fill them in and set the procedure in motion. The costs

---

Talk to the children

The most frightening thing for children whose parents are having marital problems is not knowing what is going on. If you and your partner are agreed on a separation or divorce, then let your children know as soon as you've agreed. Both of you should be there to tell them, that way there can be no unconscious attempt to align the children with either parent.

No fault

In an amicable separation or divorce, both parties consider that there is 'no fault' on either side. Generally speaking, this is a good thing, since it means that matters will be dealt with in as friendly a fashion as possible. Sometimes you need help remembering that you're being friendly, of course.

MEDIATE

If you are going for a no fault divorce, the most usual route is via the two-year separation. While you will have to go to court to get your divorce recognized by the state, it will help a lot if you have decided before then how to split your assets. There are professional mediators whose job it is to help you reach such amicable agreements. They will meet with you both a few times and suggest that, in discussions with you about children and money, you find the right way to progress through the divorce. While mediators may cost money, they will be considerably cheaper than a solicitor. Mediators cannot make legal judgements about your situation.

BE HONEST

As long as you have been honest about your financial situation when drawing up a deed of separation, and as long as you have both agreed that the terms of your separation will suffice for the divorce, everything should go smoothly. However, if you are not honest – and are found out – it can make things extremely difficult for everyone involved. So honestly declare your earnings and assets when separating, deciding on family support and so on.

AVOID COURT

Provided you both agree to the terms of the divorce and have been separated for two years, then you don't have to physically attend court in order to get a divorce made binding. As soon as you've filed your papers you have a Decree Nisi, a virtual divorce pending finalization. After 6 months or so you will get a Decree Absolute, which officially dissolves the marriage. You can now remarry.

vary, but are far less than a solicitor will charge. Involving lawyers will cost not only money, but also potentially a great deal of goodwill in terms of your relationship with your partner, too. It's in the lawyer's interests to get the 'best possible deal' for their client and while it's not intentional, the involvement of legal advisers can lead to more acrimonious proceedings than you might have wanted. Having said that, most of the DIY divorce websites do suggest that you get more legal advice than simply that contained on their forms if you have children, have been in a long (more than five years) marriage and/or have more assets to disperse than the family home and car.

Your fault divorce

If you are separating on bad terms and cannot agree on whether it's day or night, let alone money, the children or the house, you are about to go through hell. So why did you do it? Because statistically it is more likely to have been you than her who has initiated the divorce. You might not have verbally asked her for a separation, but your actions sure did.

GROUNDS FOR DIVORCE

ADULTERY

It's the single most common reason for divorce. If you are the adulterer – and the chances are that you are – then you've put yourself in an indefensible position. No matter how much you might squeal about how your wife drove you to it, that is simply

not the case. Did your wife ever tell you to go out and have sex with someone else? I don't think so. Admit it, you just couldn't keep it in your pants. Your ego, your dick and a few cheap drinks have all conspired to fuck up your marriage and put a distance between you and your kids that is going to be impossible to bridge, no matter how many happy fucking meals you buy them on a wet visiting-rights Sunday.

Don't bother denying it. It won't work. In fact it'll just make things worse. Do you really want your seedy past dragged up in court by a private eye that your wife had to hire in order to get the divorce? You will only end up paying that private dick's fees for putting on film your not so private dick's extramarital activities. So own up and be nice. It'll be better for you in the long run.

If you manage to stay in the family home with your wife and sleeping in the same bed for 6 months after your act of adultery, it's true that she cannot use your infidelity as her reason for a divorce. But don't think that you're safe. She may well still be paying that private dick to keep track of yours.

UNREASONABLE BEHAVIOUR
After mutual separation for two years and adultery, unreasonable behaviour is the next main cause of divorce. Which could be because as a description it is vague. Unreasonable behaviour can cover a multitude of sins, from violent behaviour and losing the family home in a poker game, to disappearing for long periods without explanation, being a drunk, a junkie or smelling like a rancid goat. Whatever the nature of unreasonable behaviour, it has to be explained in documents to the court, which has to accept that the behaviour as described is unreasonable.

DESERTION
This is not as common a reason for divorce as it once was. There was a time when a man would state to the family that he was going out 'to get a packet of cigarettes' and then not return. Ever. After a couple of years the wife would seek and gain a divorce. Maybe it's the fact that people don't smoke as much any more, but fewer people leave their spouse with no explanation or agreement than they used to.

SEPARATION OF FIVE YEARS OR MORE
Whether you have been apart with mutual agreement or not, after five years neither party can contest an application for divorce. They can, however, contest any final decree (division of assets, award of maintenance, etc.) on the grounds of financial or other hardship.

What if she's the adulterer?

Then you've got the moral and economic high ground. You can ask her to leave, you can keep the kids as long as they want to stay with you and, most importantly, you can be big enough to admit that it's over but that she's still their mother. While being morally in the right, you can ensure that your soon-to-be-ex-wife's relationship with your children is not wrecked.

Children and divorce

Despite the fact that the divorce rate in the UK is at its lowest for 20 years, it is still estimated that almost three out of five marriages will end in divorce. Which means that there are a lot of children with separated parents out there. Which means that there are a lot of unhappy children around. If you are ever in the situation of having to divorce, it's worth considering what your children are thinking and feeling.

The effect that divorce will have on your children will vary depending on their age, but it will always have some effect.

- **The young ones**
  No matter what you tell your children, they are going to assume that somehow

How your children might react

When you split from your partner, your children are going to go through several emotional reactions, none of them very pleasant.

SHOCK

Regardless of how long you and your partner have been shouting at each other, arguing or simply not speaking, when you make the announcement to your children that you are going to separate they will be shocked. They may say that it's good and OK, and it may even feel that way to them for a while, but shock will set in sooner or later. Your children may then start suffering illnesses that doctors can't easily diagnose, but that will be the result of the stress that your separation has brought on. They might also become quiet and withdrawn.

SHAME

Feelings of shame could be intermingled with those of guilt. Your children may know other children whose parents are divorced, but they will also know that it is not meant to be a good thing. You may have even told them to be nice to a child of a one-parent family because you feel sorry for that child. Your children will not want people to feel sorry for them; they will feel ashamed that people are, as they see it, whispering about them behind their backs because their parents are divorced.

GUILT

As I said, children will always blame themselves when parents separate. They will wonder if their naughty or noisy behaviour is what has driven daddy away (it is usually daddy who goes). They will probably ask you if you'll come home if they promise to be good. This will probably break your heart, even more than it already is.

ANGER

Do not be surprised if your child hits you, shouts at you or tells you that they hate you after you've announced your separation. This is perfectly normal. As an adult you get angry trying to deal with feelings of shock, shame and guilt, and it's no different for them. Be prepared for your child to throw things at you when you visit at weekends. Just don't throw them back. Cuddle them instead.

FEAR

Your child is going to be scared. Their world has just fallen apart. One parent has left, what's to stop the other going, too? And then what will happen to them? Will the family home be sold? Will the child have to live in another part of town or another town altogether, meaning that they'll lose all their friends as well as their family? Fear may be masked by anger or shock, but it's there.

DENIAL

Refusing to believe that the worst has happened is a common reaction to momentous events. A child may tell other people that their parents are simply living apart because of daddy's work, and may well believe it themselves. Denial may also be present in one of the parents too, of course, which will not help the child at all.

SADNESS

Your child is going to cry a lot and for a long time. Sadness may well become an ever-present emotion in the family home. Hopefully you'll cry, too.

they are the reason that their mum and dad are splitting up. Even if your children are too young to know at the time what is happening, soon they will come to believe that somehow they were to blame.

- **Teenage daydreams**
  Generally speaking, teenagers do not suffer as much emotional damage when their parents divorce as they would have done if it had happened a few years earlier (see box, below). They have spent time with both parents and if there has been a long-term problem they will be aware of it. They may even welcome the

Life is difficult and confusing enough for teenagers without having to deal with your midlife crisis, too.

split because it alleviates tension in the house. That's not to say it's going to be a good thing for your teenage children if you start an affair with a girl barely older than they are. Life is difficult and confusing enough for teenagers without having to deal with your midlife crisis, too.

Never too young to know

Whatever your child's age, if you have been present for any length of time during their early life, when you leave your child will miss you. They might not be able to vocalize that loss, but they will instinctively grieve for a lost parent. It may well be that your child takes to clinging to mum more, suffering separation anxiety more strongly than might be expected for their age. Recent research shows that children aged 5 to 9 years old are worst affected by their parents' divorce, with boys suffering the most. Children from the age of 8 upwards may show attempts to 'understand' what is happening, but of course are unable to fully comprehend the situation. Children between the ages of 10 and 12 show real anger or denial. And sometimes both.

Helping children cope

There are a number of books available that can give you more detailed advice on how best to handle your children and divorce. The following pointers are offered as basic guidelines only. As with most of the advice offered in this book, it's simple really.

KEEP TALKING

It's hugely important that you don't become estranged from your children and stop communicating with them. You have to forget any feelings of guilt or shame that you may feel and continue to try to talk to them. Do not ask them questions that they cannot answer, and that includes how they are feeling. They won't know any more than you do.

COMFORT THEM

Both parents have to keep cuddling the children, hugging them and making them feel as loved as they have ever been. Physical contact is reassuring for children and they will need physical closeness to both parents. This will help them to get over the idea that they are about to be completely abandoned.

STAY CALM

No matter what the provocation, whenever you are with the children, remain as equable as you possibly can. Do not shout at them or their mother; do not react violently if a child hits you, swears at you or throws something at you. Eventually your calm will translate to them and they too will feel that it is OK to be calm.

ASK A FRIEND

If you and your partner are having difficulty in negotiating your divorce without fights and arguments, make sure that the children are not around to witness the scene. Ask friends to take them for the hour or so that you can stand to talk things over with each other.

KEEP THEM INFORMED

The most important thing in all of this sorry mess is that you let the children know what is happening to their life and family. Do not simply walk out and not go back for days or weeks. Don't try to pretend that nothing is wrong. Treat your children with the respect that they deserve and let them know exactly what is going on. Do not pretend that you're going on holiday for a while – why can't they go? It's not fair... By keeping the truth from them you will lose their trust and respect.

Divorce dos ands don'ts

There are some things that you really must do to make sure your divorce is painless and causes the least disruption to your children's lives as possible.

DO

STAY MARRIED

Resolve your problems. It'll probably only be your vanity, ego and immaturity that need fixing. Try to keep your rampant ego and your dick in check. Go into your sleeping children's bedroom and look at them. Now ask yourself, do you really want to lose this?

BE VERY, VERY SURE

Is a divorce what you really want? It might not seem like the end of the world to you, but it will to your children. Are you sure that this isn't just a bad patch in your marriage, one that will get better? Try a separation by all means, and if it feels right being separated, then divorce – just make damned certain that divorce is the only option.

DO IT NICELY

If you cannot keep it together, then please try to be civil about things. It'll help everyone if you decide not to trade recriminations, blame or insults with your partner. It'll also be cheaper if you sort everything out without using a lawyer or solicitor.

MEDIATE

If you don't think that you and your partner can separate amicably without help, seek mediation. Mediators are professionals and will remain uninvolved. They will listen to both of you explain your situation and what you hope to achieve through the separation and divorce. They will then attempt to offer the best advice they can about what you should do. So try your best to abide by their ruling.

INVOLVE THE CHILDREN

No, that's not a joke or a mistake. Keep your children informed at every stage about what is happening. The more they know, the less they'll worry about what is going to happen.

BE FAIR

Admit what is your fault and agree on what is no one's fault. Agree on equal distribution of assets. No, scrap that, if it's you who is the adulterer, give your partner everything that she wants and needs. You can start again more easily than she can, since she's more likely to have the children living with her.

INVOLVE THE GRANDPARENTS

The immediate family needs to know that your divorce is amicable and that you are not going to be bad-mouthing your soon-to-be-ex-wife at every opportunity. By keeping both sets of grandparents involved you will lessen the chances of one sniping

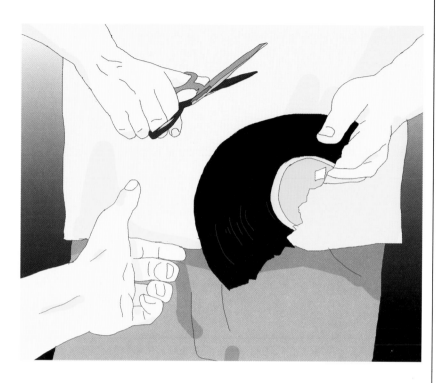

at the other or, worse still, sniping about the 'errant' parent (as they see it) to your children.

KEEP SAYING 'I LOVE YOU'

Tell your children that you love them whenever you see them. You should also tell them that you loved their mother, too, but in a different way, one that has changed now. Then reassure your children that you will always love them, no matter what. Tell them that the love of a parent for a child is the one true, never-ending love that lives happily ever after. Because it is.

BE CONSISTENT

Despite your no longer being present in the family home, when you are with your children you have to be consistent with them in the same way you were before your divorce. That means no buying them presents every weekend because you feel guilty. It means no letting them stay up late when they're with you, no giving them things that their mother doesn't allow in order to buy them off. It's unfair to their mother and to them.

Divorce dos and don'ts

DON'T

GET DIVORCED

Yes, this a repeat of the first item of advice on the previous pages, but it's worth repeating, just to make sure that you're paying attention and have thought this through properly. You are in severe danger of ruining your children's lives. That may sound extreme, but children of divorced parents are less likely to grow up to be happy, well-adjusted adults and often experience difficulty in forming fulfilling long-term relationships. Of course, many children of long-married parents have similar problems, but why take the risk of loading things against your children?

HAVE AN AFFAIR

If you are getting a divorce because of your adultery, then this advice is too late. Hopefully you are reading this before things go wrong. If so, don't have an affair. If you are in the process of separating and getting a divorce, don't have an affair. You may well be feeling lonely and there might be a willing woman close to you and available. Just hold off for a while. You are in no fit emotional state to begin anything right now, certainly not before you've properly finished the last one. Plus, your children will really not like any woman that they see you with who isn't their mother, at least not for some time. I doubt that your soon-to-be-ex-wife will like her, or you, much either.

FIGHT

Whatever the temptation, do not fight your partner over the terms of the divorce, or over visiting rights. If you cannot agree things between you, get professional help. Not necessarily a solicitor, as solicitors can feel like starting a fight that would benefit them more than you, but a mediator.

BITCH AND MOAN

About your ex-wife to anyone, especially not to your children. If you feel wronged by her, work it out with her alone. Take it to the court if you have to, but never forget that she is the mother of your children and that they love her, unconditionally. Any bitching or moaning about her is going to get back to her or your children (because these things always do) and it is only going to make a bad situation worse. Remember anger management.

RUN AWAY

Do not disappear after the divorce or separation. Do not run away and think that you have no more responsibilities towards your family. Make regular arrangements to see your children and always stick to them. Never turn up late to collect them with a lame excuse. Never even think that it's a pain to have them for a weekend. Instead consider how lucky you are that they still want to spend time with you (if they do).

ASK YOUR CHILDREN TO CHOOSE

Asking them who they want to live with is unfair and unnecessary. You are the adults, you can make the decision and they will live with it. Done properly, they need never know that there was a question over where they would live after the divorce. You should also never ask your children where they would rather spend Christmas or major holidays, post-divorce. They can have vacations with both of you at different times, which is a treat that other children don't tend to get.

USE YOUR CHILDREN TO GET INFORMATION

Do not attempt to find out about your ex-wife's life after divorce by asking your children. In fact, try not to talk about their mother with them unless absolutely necessary. Don't ask how she would do things, don't ask if they like living with her and never, ever ask if she has a boyfriend. You will be encouraging your children to lie – they will forever cling to the idea that you will be a complete family again and will say whatever they believe will make that happen.

We're a happy step-family

OKAY, YOU'VE GOT AN EX-FAMILY OF YOUR OWN, AND NOW YOU WANT
TO TAKE RESPONSIBILITY FOR ANOTHER MAN'S EX-FAMILY? GOOD LUCK!
THERE ARE AN ENORMOUS NUMBER OF STEP-FAMILIES WHO FUNCTION
WELL AND HAPPILY. BUT IT'S NOT EASY TO DO, AS YOU'RE ABOUT TO
FIND OUT . . .

Meet your step-mum

It is a common occurrence in the 21st century that no sooner does a man lose a wife than he gains another. It is just as common that on leaving a family a man finds himself living with another family, for his new partner very often has children of her own. The subject of step-families is big enough for a whole book (although, strangely, there aren't that many). The next few pages, then, are an introduction to the subject, with some general pieces of advice.

TWO MUMS?

Whether your new partner has children or not, you have and, as soon as they know about your new relationship, your children are going to start insisting that they do not have to call her 'mum'. Which is as it should be. They have only one mother and she will not be replaced. Your new partner will probably be OK with this (she's a woman, they understand better), but if she's not then you shouldn't be living with her. What are you, stupid?

DOES SHE WANT TO?

It's imperative of course that your new love wants to get to know your children and spend time with them. You are not going to give up your time with your children just because you have a sex life again, right? Neither are you going to stop taking them on holiday with you, having them stay over with you and so on. So any new love of your life, if she's to be a life partner, has to want to know and love (even if a little) your children as well as her own. We'll deal with your relationship with her children shortly.

INTRODUCTIONS

Make sure that your children meet your new partner as soon as you are both (that's you and her) sure that your relationship is serious. By serious, I mean that you intend to set up home together, whether you marry or not. It would be prudent to introduce your ex-wife to your new love before the children. If your new love has children then they should meet your children after your offspring have met her. If you think that's confusing, just wait. It gets worse.

Introductions – the ground rules

BACKGROUND

Talk your new love through your children's past history. It'll help her to relate to them better. The more that she knows about what makes them happy or sad, the better she can communicate with them and know when they are happy or sad. It's also worth discussing your ex-wife with your new love, too, but mostly as a mother.

KEEP IT FAMILIAR

For the first few meetings between your children and your new partner it's a good idea to be on neutral ground. A restaurant, cinema, swimming pool – anywhere that's not your home but is familiar to them is a good idea. It should be somewhere that you would normally go with them on your own (although not a 'special place' which is just for you and them).

You shouldn't all meet at your new love's home. Your children are going to feel awkward about meeting any other woman that you are involved with and any distraction that you can offer them will be gratefully taken. Being in public also lessens the chance of your children having a tantrum, being rude or storming off at the slightest provocation.

DON'T TOUCH

Try not to cuddle, kiss or even touch your new love in front of your children for at least the first half-dozen meetings. It's going to be hard enough for your children to come to terms with the fact that you 'love' another woman after their mother, but any physical contact between you will rub their noses in it. They might even begin to think that you and she are … having sex!

If you don't mind a cocky teenager calling you by a nickname then so be it. They can't all call you Mr X, and they won't call you uncle, so I'd suggest you let them use your first name.

Hello Step-dad

Since it's quite possible that any new woman in your life is going to have children of her own, you are about to become a step-dad. Which is kind of like being a dad, but harder. For a start, you'll probably be living with someone else's kids, not your own. And they are not going to be inclined to like you much. Especially if they have a good relationship with their biological father.

NOT MY DAD

Just as your children are going to refuse to call your new partner 'mum', so your step-children are not going to call you 'dad'. The difference here, of course, is that you are more likely to be living with your step-children than your own kids. Since mothers usually get custody of the children and the house, it will make financial and emotional sense for you to move in with her. And them. So what do they call you? If you don't mind a cocky teenager calling you by a nickname then so be it. They can't all call you Mr X, and they won't call you uncle, so I'd suggest you let them use your first name.

STEP-DAD AT HOME – THE GROUND RULES

- **Meet and greet before moving in** As with the meeting between your kids and your new love, you need to meet your potential step-children a few times on neutral ground before moving in. You also need to be there when their mother tells them that you're moving in. If your new love's husband is on good terms with her and the kids, you should meet with him before moving in and ensure that there is not going to be a problem with it. If he

can be at the announcement meeting with the kids, so much the better. (Though if he is you have to start wondering why your new love ever split up with such an understanding, straight-up nice guy.)

- **Obey her rules** When you have moved in, you may well find that your new partner has different house rules for her kids from those that you have (or had) for your own. While nothing is ever too late to try, it's probably best if you simply follow her rules, at least until you and she can discuss any ideas that you may have and then throw them out together.

- **Don't try to be cool** Remember the advice in Chapter 7. There is no such thing as a cool dad. Neither should you try to be your step-children's friend or gofer. Don't attempt to win their affections with gifts – they can see through that and though they may take them, they'll only think you're a chump for it.

- **Be yourself** Their mother fell in love with you, so why won't her kids? Oh, OK, that's just romantic bullshit. But don't attempt to be anyone other than yourself. It'll take time but they will eventually get used to you and may even come to like you a little bit.

- **Don't be a pain in the arse** You will undoubtedly be the subject of some abuse and bad language from your step-children to begin with. Ignore it.

Keep your anger in check and understand their feelings – it might be worth phoning your own children when your step-kids are being really nasty to you, just to tell them that you love them. Whatever you do, only discipline the step-children if you've agreed that you will, and what form the punishment will take, with their mother beforehand.

- **Don't touch (and for Pete's sake don't moan)**. As with the sex question and your own children, keep all physical relations with your new love to a minimum in front of the step-children, at least to begin with. By all means let them know that you love their mother, just don't flaunt your sex life in front of them. Try to keep the noise down in the bedroom, too.

Are we related?

Once you have introduced your children to your new love and she has introduced her children to you, you just have to introduce the children to each other. Phew! Usually there are only a couple of children in each family, but sometimes there are more. If you are involved in one of those step-families with multiple children, you really do need more help than you'll find here. If you're in the UK, Relate has useful advice (www.relate.org.uk) and they publish a number of books on the subject, including *The Relate Guide to Stepfamilies*. Other useful publications are *Secrets of Successful Step-families* by Sue Hart-Byers (Lothian Books, 1999) and *Step-families: Living Successfully with Other People's Children (Relate Guide)* by Suzie Hayman (Vermillion, 2001).

ARE YOU MY BROTHER?

Some children will find it confusing trying to work out who is who in a complicated domestic situation. They used to only have one mum one dad, one sibling. Now there are (possibly) two mums, two dads and three or more siblings. The grandparent situation doesn't bear thinking about. However, step-families are becoming more and more common, and your children may well have friends who are in this kind of set-up, so won't find it too strange (although they may still find it difficult).

Hopefully there will be the same number of children on each side and – even better – they'll be of roughly the same age. Hey, they might even be the same sex! In this dream-like situation it is going to be easier to integrate the step-siblings. You can introduce them to each other by their names and then tell them that they are step-brothers or step-sisters. Explain that this means they are now family. If they're old enough and angry enough about it all, they'll tell you that it's not the same as blood family. To which you simply reply in the affirmative.

STEP-SIBLINGS – THE GROUND RULES

- **Don't force it** Whatever you do, when introducing step-siblings for the first time do not tell them that they have to be friends, or that they should be. You may have noticed that your kids are particularly averse to being told what to do by you since the divorce. One possible approach could be to tell your kids that they'll hate the others and let reverse psychology take over.

- **Be neutral** It's unfair on your children to make them meet their step-siblings on foreign territory. So, as you did when you met your new partner's kids for the first time, get everyone to meet for the first time at an 'occasion' and on neutral

You may have noticed that your kids are particularly averse to being told what to do by you since the divorce.

Who's who?

Step-family trees can be complex beasts. A typical one might look like this. A jagged line indicates a marriage that ended in divorce (for example Tom and Lesley Porter). A straight line indicates remarriage (for example, Lesley Porter to Jim Robins).

1 Tom is Mary's step-dad

2 Leon is Josie's step-brother

3 Sarah is Alice's step-mum

4 Ben is Barbara's half-brother
(i.e. they have a parent in common)

5 Josie is Barbara's half-sister

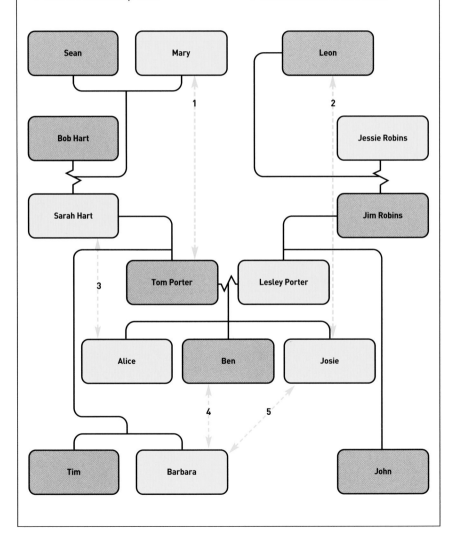

Make sure that you have established ground rules for behaviour with all of them before the meeting (no kicking, spitting or eye gouging, perhaps?) and also told them what punishments will be handed out for any breaking of the rules.

ground. Make it a trip to somewhere that everyone will enjoy and where there's a chance that some activity or other will so engross the kids that they'll end up doing things together and playing together naturally. Obviously this is more tricky with teenagers. In this case you could meet at a restaurant or bar. If one set of siblings is much older than the others it could be good, though. The older ones (especially if girls) will hopefully feel protective towards their new little sisters or brothers.

- **Show no prejudice** When your children meet up, you have to treat all of them equally and show no favouritism. Neither should you be especially hard on your own kids in order to show your step-kids that you are 'fair'. Make sure that you have established ground rules for behaviour with all of them before the meeting (no kicking, spitting or eye gouging, perhaps?) and also told them what punishments will be handed out for any breaking of the rules.

- **Have fun** Try to do something that is going to be fun for both the kids and for you. There's no point going to a game if half the kids hate the sport. And there's no gain to be had from forcing them to trudge around a science museum if they would rather be roller-blading or flying a kite. Enabling children to laugh together is a great bonding tool. It doesn't have to be big or clever; the outing could simply be a trip to the local multiplex for a movie and then something to eat. Behave as if it's someone's birthday and make sure that you get the kids interacting with each other.

- **Be regular** Once the ice is broken and the step-siblings have met and (hopefully) got on, then you can begin to have regular get-togethers. And they should be regular. Once a month at least, twice is better and weekly is great as long as it's going OK. And then don't make it compulsory. If the step-siblings get along and have fun on their trips out together they'll want to go anyway. Before long you can start inviting them to each other's houses. Just as long as the other step-mum and step-dad don't mind, of course.

All under one roof

Now that everyone in the step-family knows each other, it's time to start spending time together under the same roof. Since you live with your step-kids, you'll have to work out how to get your biological children integrated into your new life with the least hassle.

DON'T RUSH IT

Just because you've had a couple of good weekends where all the kids have played well together and no one's been too badly hurt, it doesn't mean that your children are ready to start spending weekends with their step-siblings. These things take time. If you can, wait until your kids ask for a sleepover at your new home, and if they do it will be because they want to spend time with their step-siblings as well as you.

Sometimes, the step-siblings may be getting on too well. This is another reason to take your time. Bonds can form too quickly between kids who have something of a shared history. While it's great that the two sets of children get on well, it's important that you understand the nature of that bond and are sure that they are not forming a team in order to attempt to break up your current relationship. Remember that your kids, and your new partners, will always believe that their real parents will one day reunite and so will do whatever they think it takes to bring that about.

DON'T TAKE SIDES

You have to treat every child in your house as if they are yours. As tempting as it may be to favour your own offspring over your step-children, don't. It's not fair on either family.

Neither should you be harder on your kids than on your step-children. Same result as being easier on them – resentment. So how do you do this?

MAKE A FEW RULES

You and your partner need to set house rules for the children and make sure that you both stick to them. It would be useful if you could also get your ex-wife and your partner's ex-husband to agree to the same rules, although that won't be plain sailing. As I've said before, children need consistency and stability in order to thrive. They've lost a lot of stability because of your divorce, so help them by keeping to the rules.

- **Set out the major rules** Bed times (different schedules for different ages, of course), meal times, what kind of behaviour is forbidden (swearing, hitting, drug-taking), the rota for chores, the time set for homework and so on. Paste up a list somewhere in the house so that it's always visible.

- **Be realistic** Don't make harsh and unbendable rules simply to be authoritative. Think about what is going to be accomplished by enforcing the house rules and whether your children are old enough to be able to follow them. Explain why the rules are there, and if you have no good reason for any rule to be in place, don't use it.

- **Ignore minor naughtiness** That means squabbles over who gets to watch what

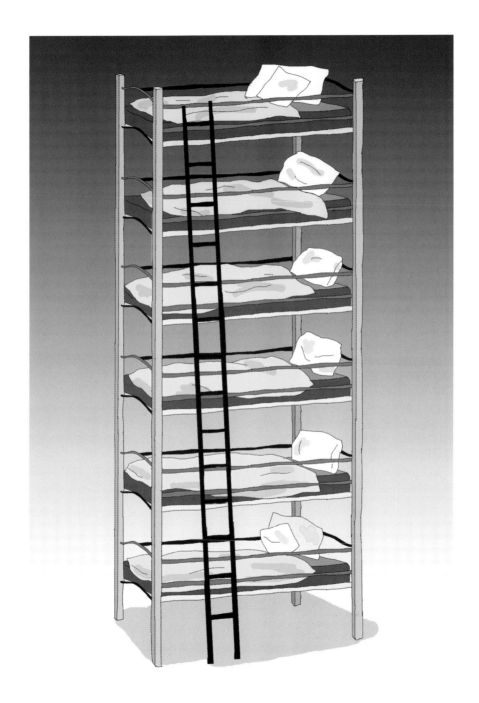

on TV, who stole whose toy, who broke what. Teach the children how to negotiate. On the matter of DVD or TV watching, suggest that three (or five) choices are offered and the majority vote wins the viewing. You could also explain the basics of modern Western democracy while you're at it.

- **Never argue** Not with the children and not with your partner. At least not where and when the children can hear you. If your partner and you are about to argue, take it outside, to the car or the garage or the garden. If it's freezing cold, that's good. The argument will fizzle out pretty quickly. Children learn their behaviour from you, so, hopefully, when they want to argue, they'll take it outside, too, with the same kind of results. There's every chance that your last marriage failed amid a sea of arguments that your children will have witnessed. If they see it happening again, they'll start to think the worst. And that's not happening, is it? Well, is it?

- **Don't make the kids share rooms** Not always possible, of course, but it's not a good idea to make your step-children move out of their rooms or beds in order to accommodate a new child. Face it, if there's not enough room at your new

home to take all of the kids, you shouldn't do it. It's no good you assuaging your guilt by (as you see it) taking on extra responsibility if the children are simply going to be cramped and miserable.

WHAT IF IT ALL GOES WRONG?

If you and/or your partner feel a sense of dread as the Friday approaches when all the kids are due to be together under your roof, there is a very good chance that one, some or all of the children are feeling the same way. So you have to ask yourself if it is really worth it. If all the children do is fight, whine, sulk and complain, and if all you and your partner do is shout, order, sulk and complain, then the answer is no, it's not worth it.

So stop.

OK, so this is not the usual, right-on approach to the problem. But really, is there any point in continuing with the farce of pretending that your kids and those of your new partner are going to be one big, happy family if all you can do is have a bad time while you are together? So accept that it's not working this time, this way. See your kids somewhere else. By all means have them come to the house for short periods, just don't force them to stay over. And remember, just because it hasn't worked to begin with, that doesn't mean it never will. Just don't force it. Infrequent visits and less time spent together can often give rise to a desire for

Do not discuss 'mum' unless they want to and, if they start complaining about her, refrain from looking smug and encouraging their complaints.

Why didn't it work?

Well, ask yourself. You may want to blame the children, and, after all, that's the easy option. But who's in charge here? Are there things you could have done differently that would have made those weekends together more of a success?

DID YOU PRY?

All your questions about how your kids live their life now that you're not there every day might have been asked in the spirit of genuine interest on your part, but they seemed like prying to your kids. After all, you didn't care enough about their everyday lives to stick around while they were growing up, did you? Talk about their school or extracurricular activities only if they volunteer information. Don't start asking how their week was when they get to your place. Often they can't remember anyway, so don't push it.

DID YOU DISS THEIR MUM?

Or use them as spies to gather information for you? They love their mother even if you don't, and she spends far more time with them than you do. Do not discuss 'mum' unless they want to and, if they start complaining about her, refrain from looking smug and encouraging their complaints. Defend your ex-wife's behaviour as much as possible to them and, if it really sounds as if there is a problem between her and your children, talk to her about it, not them.

WERE YOU EVEN-HANDED?

If you are all playing games together, whether it's football, tag or Monopoly, don't favour your kids, don't compete with them and don't encourage any one child over the others. Your kids will be looking for any further proof that you don't love them and it's easy during the heat of a game to vent strong negative emotions. If it happens, then either ignore it or, if it involves breaking a major house rule, put the child out of the game to calm down and then let them back in.

the opposite. Allow your children to come to the idea in their own time.

HOW IT MIGHT WORK OUT

If you can control your own emotions, feelings and temper, things will eventually work out between you, your children and your step-family. If you have set rules that all the adults agree to, then it will work. Most importantly, though, if you all manage to have at least an hour's fun over the long weekend that everyone is under the same roof, then it will work out. Do things together as much as possible, especially eating, playing and laughing. How you make each other happy is the most important thing to discover and then keep doing. So set to it.

Happy endings?

Does anyone ever manage a happy ending? Do they really live happily ever after? The encouraging answer is yes, some people do. Of course, it's not everyone. Some people seem to collect step-families as if they're playing a card game. Others lose contact with their biological children for ever once they've left the marital home. Most of those who do are male, of course.

Why?

Because men find it easier to run away than to face their own failings, and seeing the

lost, hurt look on your child's face every time that you drop them back at home after even the dullest, wettest afternoon spent together is a constant reminder of your failings.

ACCEPT RESPONSIBILITY – BE A MAN

Sure, you can blame the kid's mother, you can blame the government, the courts and even God if you want to, but deep down, as a divorced dad, you have to recognize that you must shoulder most of the blame. Putting on silly costumes and climbing onto public buildings in order to blame the system is not going to make your relationship with your child any better. But it will make you look like the loser that you are.

If you are unfortunate enough to be an estranged dad, please do not rage at everything and anything that you can as being the cause of your misery. Doing that only shows your immaturity. It is most likely nobody's fault but yours. Even if the mother of your child was at fault for the collapse of the relationship, accept that you share the responsibility for the happiness and well-being of your child.

MAKE IT BETTER

Once you've taken responsibility for the failure of your marriage or relationship with the mother of your children, then you can start to move on. Eventually you will be able to look your child in the eye and see not failure but the potential to be happy. If you cannot keep your relationship with the mother of your children on track, make sure that you stay close to your children. They need you. No matter how fucked up you are or how bad your life is, your children see you, their dad, as a hero. Just because it's a cliché doesn't make it any less true.

Putting on silly costumes and climbing onto public buildings in order to blame the system is not going to make your relationship with your child any better.

If you find love with another woman and take on the responsibility of more children, your biological children will be jealous and hurt. But it won't last. If you are happy then they will eventually be happy for you. As long as you can keep your relationships together you are giving your children the best possible advantage in life, because your example will have a huge impact on their future lives.

BE HAPPY

If you are happy, so will your children be.

After they've gone

Actually, they never leave. Your children will be there for the rest of your life. If not in your house, certainly in your thoughts, your mind and often your bank account, too. They may well stay at home with you for longer than you lived in your own parents' home, since the idea of home ownership for young adults today is an almost impossible dream, with property prices and rental costs having increased exponentially in most of the Western world. If your child gets to live on campus at university, then good for them, that's an experience they should have.

However, after college and before getting a sufficiently well-paid job, increasing numbers of people aged up to 30 are now staying at home with their parents. Until they have jobs which pay them enough to allow them not to be mortgaged up to their eyeballs, your children will be able to enjoy a better quality of life by staying with you – even if you make them pay a nominal rent – than they would if they entered the commercial property market.

The fact that your kids may want to stay at home when they're adults is great in one way. They like you, and you are obviously on good terms with them, or they would have found any way they could to get out, from sleeping on a friend's floor to paying their entire wage over to a landlord in rent.

However, it is a good idea for them to leave your home at some point. You should have instilled a sense of independence in them at an early age. Not that they should have been changing their own nappies or anything, but you did allow your kids to stay over at friend's houses or go on properly organized trips in their early teen years, didn't you?

Ooops, sorry. Should have told you that earlier I guess.

If you are still making meals for a 30-year-old, then I think we can safely say that child has problems that need addressing.

> # If you are still making meals for a 30-year-old, then I think we can safely say that child has problems that need addressing.

HELLO GRANDPA

If you're lucky, you might get a few years between your children leaving home and the time they begin to drop their babies off at your place for babysitting duty. You should spend that time doing as much travelling and other leisure pursuits as you can. Because when you become a grandparent it all starts again. You'll be holidaying with your kids and their kids, having grandchildren to stay over for weekends and staying over at theirs when called for.

You might want to go back over the sections in this book that deal with relations between sons and dads and grandparents, but this time reading it from a different perspective – that of the grandfather.

BE PREPARED

You will probably be called upon to give financial aid to your children when they are adults. In fact, you will never stop giving them financial aid. So the more that you can put away now for that eventuality the better. Any kind of policy that matures when you're past retirement age is good. Something that pays a lump sum can give you and your kids a nice financial surprise in a few years' time.

You should probably resist the urge to move to a smaller house when all of the kids have left home, because they'll be back at some point. Probably with more additions to your family, so you'll need all of those bedrooms.

ENJOY

By the time your kids have left home you should know that having a family is the greatest achievement of your life. Knowing that you have children who are happy, healthy and who love you is a far, far greater reward than any kind of business deal made or financial target met. So spend as much time as you can with your family, and truly enjoy your life.

Further reading

GENERAL PREGNANCY GUIDES

What To Expect When You're Expecting
Arlene Eisenberg
Simon & Schuster

What To Expect The First Year
Arlene Eisenberg
Simon & Schuster

The Best Friend's Guide To Pregnancy: Or Everything Your Doctor Won't Tell You
Vicki Iovine
Bloomsbury

MEN'S HEALTH

A Bloke's Diagnose It Yourself Guide to Health
Keith Hopcroft & Alistair Moulds
Bloomsbury

The Complete Guide to Men's Health
The American Medical Association
Rodale Press (USA)

The Man's Body: An Owner's Manual
Wordsworth Editions

Men's Health Matters: The Complete A-Z of Male Health
Nikki Bradford
Vermillion

Real Health For Men
Peter Baker
Vega

MEN'S PARENTING

What To Expect When Your Wife's Expanding
Thomas Hill, Patrick Merell
Andrews McMeel

Baby: Conception to Two Years
Owners Workshop Manual
Haynes

PARENTING

Babies For Beginners
Roni Jay
White Ladder Press

The Parent/Child Game
Sue Jenner
Bloomsbury

The Complete Secrets of Happy Children: A Guide for Parents
Steve Biddulph, Sharon Biddulph
HarperCollins

STEP-PARENTING

Secrets of Successful Step-Families
Sue Hart-Byers
Lothian Books

Step Families: Living Successfully With other People's Children (Relate Guide)
Suzi Hayman
Vermillion

Check it out – answers

OK, so not all the answers are here, but really, did you honestly think these were serious questions!? Well, some of them were. See below.

THE SCIENCE OF CONCEPTION

True or False The vas deferens is a new German luxury saloon car. F

True or False A woman has two fallopian tubes. T

True or False You know exactly where the fallopian tubes are. **Er...**

HOW TO DO IT NATURALLY

True or False The chances of getting pregnant in the first month of trying are better than in the 18th month. F

Ovulation occurs on day 7, day 14, day 21, day 28, whenever she says it does.

day 14

The optimum amount of alcohol that a woman should drink while attempting to conceive is 1 unit a day, I unit a week, whatever gets her drunk.

1 per day

The optimum amount of alcohol that a man should drink while attempting to impregnate a woman is 21 units a day, 21 units a week, whatever gets him going. **21 a week**

HOW TO DO IT WITH HELP

True or False An ultrasound scan hurts. F

TESTING TIME

True or False Antenatal care isn't actually against anything. T

True or False The triple test only happens once. T

True or False Amniocentesis, CVS and UVS carry a small chance of harming the baby. T

BUILDING A NEST

True or False You need at least two bedrooms in your home. T

IN CASE YOU WERE WONDERING

True or False All geniuses listen to Bach while in their mother's womb.

F It's Mozart, dummy!

Index